NEW HORIZONS IN ENGLISH is a communication-centered, six-level, basal series planned and written to make the learning of English as a second language effective and rewarding. Stimulating opportunities to practice listening, speaking, reading, and writing skills develop independence and confidence in the use of English. Thoughtfully chosen vocabulary gives students the words they need to communicate in their new language in a variety of situations; carefully paced introduction of grammatical and structural concepts helps insure a strong foundation of communication skills.

Important to every learner is a sense of achievement, a feeling that he or she has successfully accomplished the tasks presented. Motivation, the desire to learn, is equally important. NEW HORIZONS IN ENGLISH is written to satisfy both needs: to provoke, through selection of topics, vocabulary, and illustrations, a genuine interest in learning more, and to pace and schedule material in such a way that achievement and mastery are facilitated. The content moves in systematic small steps, never overwhelming the learner, and each step is reinforced from unit to unit and level to level, in combination with new material. The progression of learning is planned, sequential, and cumulative. There is minimum potential for error and maximum potential for easy, satisfying mastery.

The language used in NEW HORIZONS IN ENGLISH is contemporary and relevant. Most important, it is English that students can and will use outside the classroom. Natural exchanges and dialogues arise from the real-life situations that form unit themes. Readings and written exercises are related to these themes, rounding out each unit. A strong listening strand, running throughout the series, builds student ability to derive meaning, both explicit and implicit, from spoken material. The emphasis on speaking and listening, with meaning always paramount, means that oral communicative competence develops early and is broadened and deepened as students move through the series. Parallel development of reading and writing skills promotes competence in other communication areas at the same time.

Dialogues and readings from the texts, and many of the exercises, are recorded on the optional tape cassette program, which provides models of American pronunciation and intonation. Separate pronunciation exercises in the first and second books help students associate particular consonant and vowel sounds (always in the context of words) with their English spellings.

Each level of NEW HORIZONS IN ENGLISH includes a workbook to provide additional practice and application of skills and vocabulary introduced in the text. A series of picture cards, the NEW HORIZONS IN ENGLISH PICTURE SHOW, may be used to help present vocabulary and generate conversation. An associated series, *Skill Sharpeners 1-4*, includes a variety of exercises and activities that further reinforce and extend the skills and concepts taught in NEW HORIZONS IN ENGLISH.

A complete program to build communicative competence, NEW HORIZONS IN ENGLISH provides motivation, mastery, and a sense of achievement. Every student—and every teacher—needs the feeling of pride in a job well done. NEW HORIZONS IN ENGLISH, with its unbeatable formula for classroom success, insures that this need will be filled.

CONTENTS

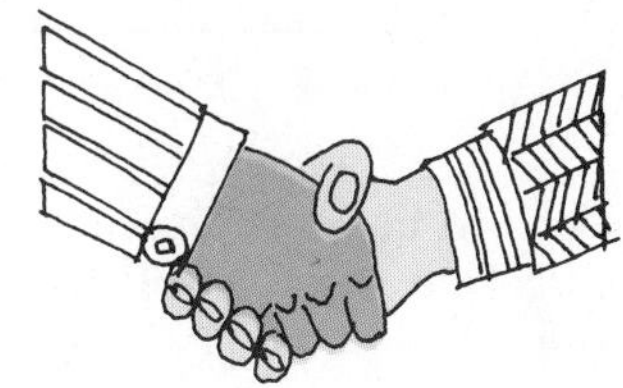

PLANE SCHEDULE
WA 602
TO JAPAN
12P.M.

NEW HORIZONS IN ENGLISH 1

SECOND EDITION

UNIT 1 ONE

Hi, Mary!
Hello, Ben.

This is my friend Peter.
Pleased to meet you.
Glad to meet *you*.
Good-bye.
So long.

Hi, what's your name?
My name is Mary.
What's *your* name?
My name is Tom.
1.
What's her name?
Her name is Lucy.
2.
Lucy, this is my
friend Tom.
Hello, Tom.
Pleased to meet you.
Hello, Lucy.
Glad to meet *you*.
3.

4.
What's his name?
His name is Don.
5.
Don, this is my friend Mary.
Hello, Mary.
Pleased to meet you.
Hello, Don.
Glad to meet *you*.
6.
Good morning, Mary.
Good morning, Lucy.
So long!
See you later!
7.
Hello, Don!
Hi, Jack.
See you later!
Bye.

What's her name?	**Mary**	**Her name is Mary.**

1. What's her name? Lucy Her name is Lucy.
2. What's her name? Carmen Her name is Carmen.
3. What's her name? Sally Her name is Sally.

What's his name?	**Ben**	**His name is Ben.**

1. What's his name? Mike His name is Mike.
2. What's his name? Don His name is Don.
3. What's his name? Peter His name is Peter.

1. What's his name? His name is Ben.
2. What's her name? Her name is Lucy.
3. What's her name? Her name is Mary.
4. What's his name? His name is Peter.
5. What's her name? Her name is Carmen.
6. What's his name? His name is Mike.
7. What's her name? Her name is Sally.
8. What's his name? His name is Don.

—Good morning, Tom.
—Good morning, Mary. Is his name John?
—No, it isn't.
—Well, what *is* it?
—It's Fred.

1. 
—Is his name Ben?
—Yes, it is.

2. 
—Is his name John?
—No, it isn't.

3. 
—Is his name Peter?
—No, it isn't.
—Well, what *is* it?
—It's Mike.

4. 
—Is his name Don?
—No, it isn't.
—Well, what *is* it?
—It's Jack.

5. 
—Is her name Lucy?
—Yes, it is.

6. 
—Is her name Susan?
—No, it isn't.

7. 
—Is her name Carmen?
—No, it isn't.
—Well, what *is* it?
—It's Sally.

8. 
—Is her name Mary?
—No, it isn't.
—Well, what *is* it?
—It's Carmen.

LISTEN & UNDERSTAND

BASICS

STATEMENTS:	His name is Tom. It's Tom.
SHORT ANSWERS:	Yes, it is. No, it isn't.
YES-NO QUESTION:	Is his name Tom?
INFORMATION QUESTIONS:	What's his name? What is it?

CONTRACTIONS:

what is → what's
it is → it's
is not → isn't

POSSESSIVE ADJECTIVES:

This is **my** / **your** / **his** / **her** friend.

VOCABULARY/EXPRESSIONS

friend
her
his
is
it
my
name
no
this
what
yes
you
your

Bye.
Glad to meet you.
Good-bye.
Good morning.
Hello.
Hi.
Pleased to meet you.
See you later.
So long.
Well...

UNIT 2 TWO
20% OFF
SALE "HATS"
Excuse me. That's my hat.
Oh no it isn't!
Yes it *is*!
No it ISN'T!
Excuse me. That's my hat.
Oh. Sorry!
Excuse me.

What's this?  It's a hat.

1. Is this a hat? 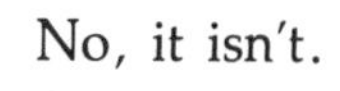 No, it isn't.
2. Is this a sweater? 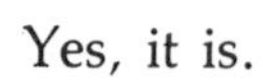 Yes, it is.
3. Is this a blouse? Yes, it is.
4. Is this a tie? No, it isn't.
5. Is this a shirt? Yes, it is.
6. Is this a dress? Yes, it is.

1.
This is her scarf.
That is her sweater.
2.
This is his tie.
That is his shirt.
3.
This is her dress.
That is her blouse.
4.
This is his hat.
That is his suit.

What's your favorite color?

It's blue.

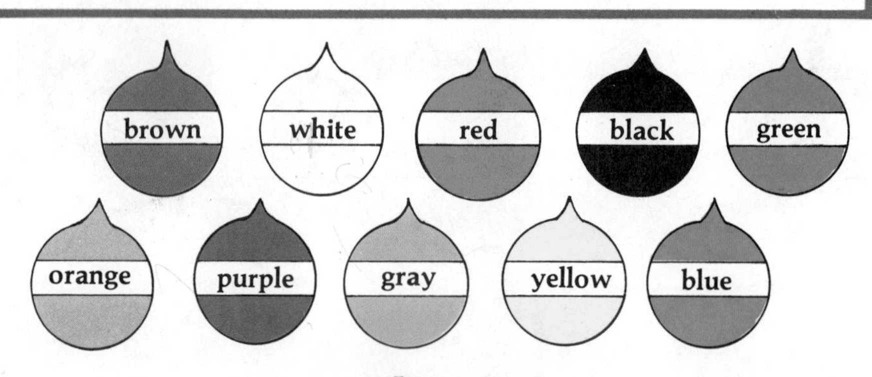

1. What color is his shirt?

   It's white.

2. What color is her hat?

   It's gray.

3. What color is his suit?

   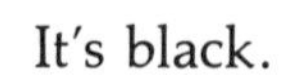

   It's black.

4. What color is his bathrobe?

   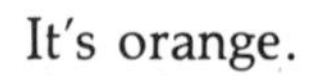

   It's orange.

5. What color is her skirt?

   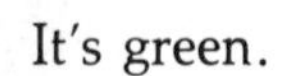

   It's green.

6. What color is his jacket?

   It's yellow.

What color are his shoes?

They're brown.

1. What color are his slacks?

They're green.

2. What color are his shorts?

They're white.

3. What color are his socks?

They're blue.

4. What color are her boots?

They're black.

5. What color are her slippers?

They're yellow.

6. What color are her jeans?

They're red.

7. What color are her glasses?

They're orange.

What's he wearing?		**He's wearing a brown tie.**

1. What's he wearing? — He's wearing a green shirt.

2. What's she wearing? — She's wearing a red blouse.

3. What's she wearing? — She's wearing a yellow sweater.

What's s(he) wearing?

What's he wearing?		He's wearing white shorts.

1. What's she wearing?  She's wearing green socks.

2. What's he wearing?  He's wearing black boots.

3. What's she wearing? 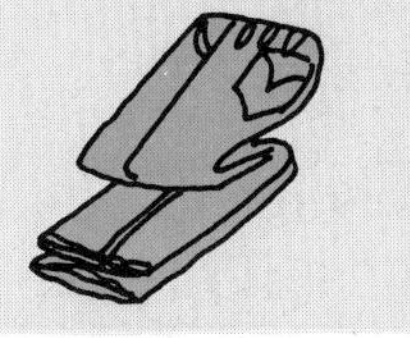 She's wearing blue slacks.

What's s(he) wearing?

Joe is wearing a blue hat.

Sally is wearing a black sweater.

Koko is wearing yellow shoes.

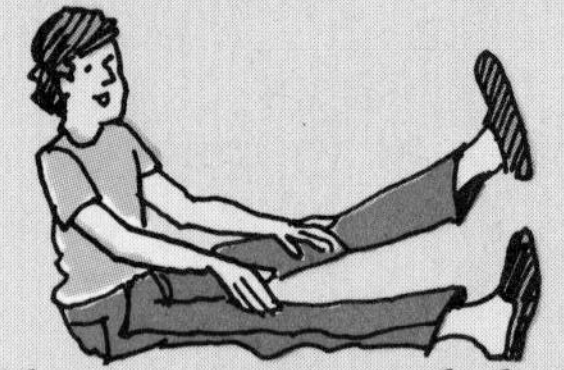

Mike is wearing red slacks.

1. Who's wearing a blue hat?	Joe is.
2. Who's wearing a black sweater?	Sally is.
3. Who's wearing yellow shoes?	Koko is.
4. Who's wearing red slacks?	Mike is.

---

1. Is Mike wearing a red hat?	No, he isn't.
2. Is Mike wearing red slacks?	Yes, he is.
3. Is Sally wearing a red sweater?	No, she isn't.
4. Is Sally wearing a black sweater?	Yes, she is.
5. Is Mike wearing a red hat, or red slacks?	He's wearing red slacks.
6. Is Koko wearing a yellow blouse, or yellow shoes?	She's wearing yellow shoes.
7. Is Joe wearing a blue hat, or a blue tie?	He's wearing a blue hat.
8. Is Sally wearing a black sweater or a black skirt?	She's wearing a a black sweater.

LISTEN & UNDERSTAND

PRONUNCIATION

I. Hello.

Hello, what's your name?

My name is Ben. What's *your* name?

It's Sally.

II. Is your name Carmen?

Is his name Peter?

Is her name Sally or Lucy?

Is she wearing a dress or a bathrobe?

III. Is your name Mike?

No, it isn't. It's Tom.

Who's wearing a red hat?

Koko is.

Who's wearing shorts?

Peter is.

What color are his shorts?

They're white.

IV. Is he wearing a green tie, or a brown tie?

He's wearing a green tie.

Is she wearing shoes or boots?

She's wearing boots.

Is this your jacket?

No, *that's* my jacket.

STATEMENT:	Joe is wearing a blue hat.
CHOICE QUESTION:	Is he wearing a blue hat, or a red hat?
INFORMATION QUESTIONS:	What's he wearing? Who's wearing shorts? What color is his tie? What color are his shoes? What's this?

ADJECTIVES:

	red	
Bill is wearing a	**white**	shirt.
	green	

	brown	
Judy is wearing	**black**	boots.
	orange	

TO BE FORMS:

What color **is** his hat?	His hat **is** brown.
What color **are** his shorts?	They **are** white.

DEMONSTRATIVE PRONOUNS:

This is her hat.

That is his hat.

BASICS

PRONOUNS:

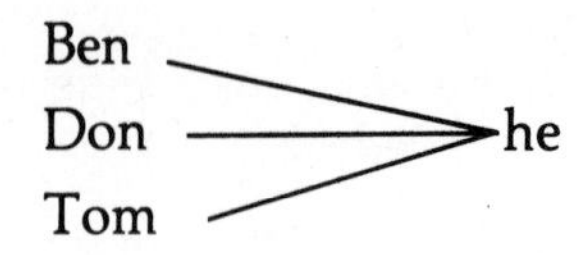

Carmen, Lucy, Mary → she

hat, sweater, bathrobe → it

shorts, glasses, shoes → they

CONTRACTIONS:

that is → that's
who is → who's

he is → he's
she is → she's
they are → they're

VOCABULARY/EXPRESSIONS

a
are
bathrobe
belt
black
blouse
blue
boots
brown
color
dress
favorite
glasses
gray
green
hat(s)
he
jacket
jeans
or
orange
purple
raincoat
red
scarf
she
shirt
shoes
shorts
skirt
slacks
slippers
socks
suit
sweater
that
they
tie
wearing
white
who
yellow

Excuse me.
Oh no it isn't.
Oh. Sorry!

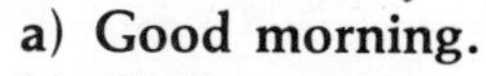

I. 1. Hello, Lucy.
This is my friend Tom.

a) **Good morning.**
b) **Glad to meet you.**
c) **See you later.**

2. See you later.

a) **Good morning.**
b) **Yes, it is.**
c) **Good-bye.**

3. What's **a) his** / **b) her** / **c) your** name?

My name is Mary.

4. Is **a) his** / **b) her** name Jack?

No, it isn't.

Well, what is it?

a) **It's Tom.**
b) **What's Tom?**
c) **This is my friend.**

5. What's Bill wearing?

a) **He's**
b) **She's** wearing a jacket.
c) **It's**

6. What color is her blouse?

It's **a) red.** / **b) yellow.** / **c) white.**

7. What color is his bathrobe?

It's **a) orange.** / **b) green.** / **c) blue.**

8. What color are her shoes?

They're **a) black.** / **b) brown.** / **c) purple.**

9. What color are his slacks?

a) It's / **b) He's** / **c) They're** green.

II.

1. What's Sue wearing?

2. What's Bob wearing?

1. a hat
2. a sweater
3. socks
4. a blouse
5. a shirt
6. a skirt
7. a tie
8. a jacket
9. shoes
10. boots
11. a raincoat
12. shorts
13. glasses
14. slacks
15. slippers

III.

1. What's her name?	. . . .
2. . . . . ?	His name is Tom.
3. . . . . Peter?	No, it isn't.
4. What's this?	. . . . a green shirt.
5. Is this your hat?	No, ... My hat is green.
6. . . . . wearing a red sweater?	Don is.
7. . . . . a red raincoat?	Yes, she is.

UNIT 3 THREE

Where's my jacket?
It's on the sofa.
Where's my raincoat?
It's in the bedroom.
Where are my boots?
They're under the chair.

Where's the tie?
It's on the table.

Where's the hat?
It's on the chair.

Where's the belt?
It's under the chair.

Where's the shirt?
It's under the table.

1. Where's the raincoat?  It's on the chair.

2. Where's the bathrobe?  It's under the table.

3. Where's the scarf?  It's on the bed.

4. Where's the sweater?  It's under the sofa.

Lucy is in her bedroom.
Her hat is on the chair.
Her blouse is on the table.
Her scarf is on the floor.
Her bathrobe is on the bed.
Her slippers are on the rug.

1. Where's her hat?	It's on the chair.
2. Where's her blouse?	It's on the table.
3. Where's her scarf?	It's on the floor.
4. Where's her bathrobe?	It's on the bed.
5. Where are her slippers?	They're on the rug.

Ben is in the living room.
His shirt is on the sofa.
His tie is on the chair.
His belt is on the table.
His socks are on the lamp.
His shoes are on the rug.

1. What's on the sofa?
2. What's on the chair?
3. What's on the table?
4. What are on the lamp?
5. What are on the rug?

What time is it?

1. It's one o'clock.

2. It's two o'clock.

3. It's three o'clock.

4. It's quarter to four.

5. It's quarter to five.

6. It's quarter past six.

7. It's quarter past seven.

8. It's half past eight.

9. It's half past nine.

10. It's ten-thirty.

11. It's eleven-thirty.

12. It's twelve o'clock. It's noon.

13. It's twelve o'clock. It's midnight.

What time is it now?

1.

2.

3.

AT THE BUS STOP

1.

2.

—Excuse me, what time is it?
—It's one o'clock.
—When is the next bus?
—I'm sorry, I don't know.

3.

—Excuse me, what time is it?
—It's half past one.
—When is the next bus?
—I'm sorry, I don't know.

4.

—Excuse me, what time is it?
—It's quarter to two.
—When is the next bus?
—I'm sorry, I don't know.

5.

Mr. Jones Mrs. Rivera Mr. King Miss Black

Mr. Jones is in front of Mrs. Rivera.
Mrs. Rivera is in front of Mr. King.
Mr. King is in front of Miss Black.

Miss Black Mr. King Mrs. Rivera Mr. Jones

Mrs. Rivera is behind Mr. Jones.
Mr. King is behind Mrs. Rivera.
Miss Black is behind Mr. King.

Tom			Mary.
Mary		in front of	Bill.
Joe			Sally.
	is		
Lucy			Jack.
Peter		behind	Lucy.
Carmen			Peter.

	Tom?		
Where's	Joe?	He's	in front of...
	Peter?		
	Mary?		
Where's	Lucy?	She's	behind...
	Carmen?		

LISTEN & UNDERSTAND

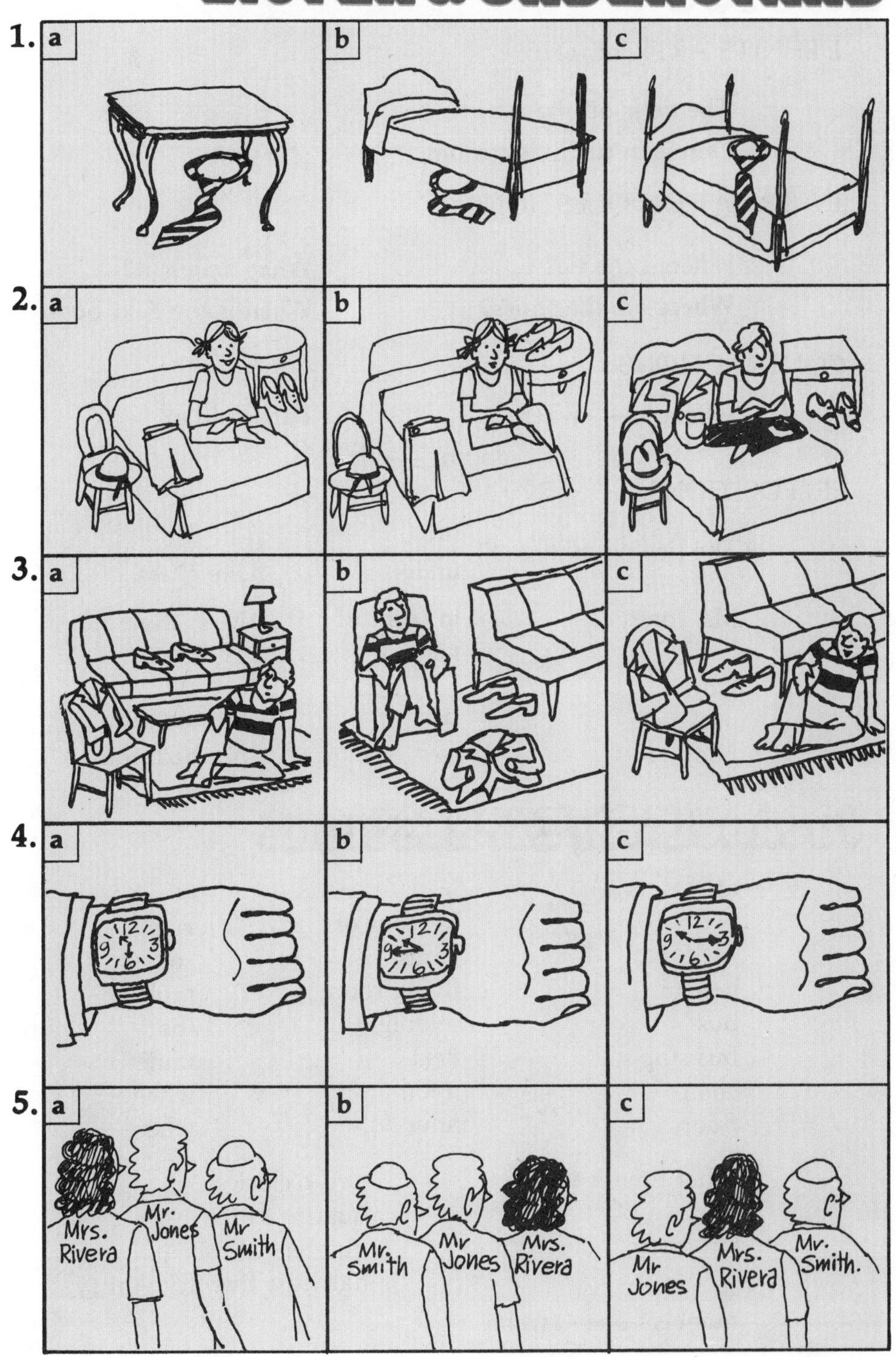

BASICS

DEFINITE ARTICLE THE:

The tie is on **the** table.
Don is in **the** living room.

INFORMATION QUESTIONS:

Where's the tie?
Where are the shoes?

What time is it?
When is the next bus?

CONTRACTIONS:

where is ⟶ where's
I am ⟶ I'm
do not ⟶ don't

PREPOSITIONS:

The tie		**on** / **under**	the chair.
Mr. Jones	is	**in front of** / **behind**	Mrs. Rivera.
Don		**at**	the bus stop.
Lucy		**in**	her bedroom.

VOCABULARY/EXPRESSIONS

at
bed
bedroom
behind
bus
bus stop
chair
floor
in
in front of
lamp
living room
midnight
next
noon
now
on
rug
sofa
table
the
under
when
where

What time is it?

I'm sorry, I don't know.

two o'clock
quarter to ten
quarter past six
half past five (five-thirty)

numbers one - twelve

—Who's that boy?
—Who?
—The boy in the green pants.
—Oh, that's Joe.

—Who's that girl?
—Who?
—The girl in the blue dress.
—Oh, that's Jane.

1. Who's this?
   How old is she?
   What color is her hair?
   Is she thin or chubby?
   And what color are her eyes?

It's Lucy.
She's nineteen.
It's black.
She's chubby.
They're black.

2. Who's this?
   How old is he?
   What color is his hair?
   Is he tall or short?
   And what color are his eyes?

It's Daniel.
He's thirteen.
It's blond.
He's short.
They're green.

3. Who's this?
   How old is **he**?
   What color is **his** hair?
   What color are **his** eyes?
   Is **he** thin or chubby?
   Is he tall or short?

It's **Bill.**
He's fourteen.
It's **red.**
They're **blue.**
He's chubby.
He's tall.

—Look at that **woman** over there.

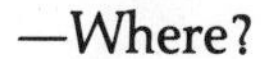

—Where?

—There—the **woman in the red dress.**

—Oh, that's **Elena.**

—What's **her** last name?

—It's **Rivera.**

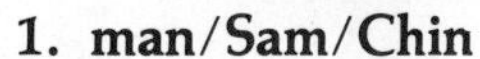

1. man/Sam/Chin

2. boy/Tim/Novak

—Look, this is Ted.

—Is he your new boyfriend?

—Yes, he is.

—What's he like?

—Well, he's thin. His hair is red, and his eyes are green. He's very tall and handsome. And he's seventeen.

—Look, this is Rita.

—Is she your new girl friend?

—Yes, she is.

—What's she like?

—Well, she's short and chubby. Her hair is blonde, and her eyes are blue. She's fifteen, and very pretty!

Who's this?
What's **his** last name?
How old is **he**?
Is **he** tall or short?
Is **he** chubby or thin?
What color is **his** hair?
What's **he** wearing?

It's Frank.
It's Mann.
He's twenty.
He's short.
He's thin.
It's brown.
He's wearing
a white shirt,
a gray tie,
a blue jacket,
brown slacks and
black shoes.

Frank Mann

1. Joe Nunez
2. Susie Wong
3. Tim Grubb
4. Pat Pratt

LISTEN & UNDERSTAND

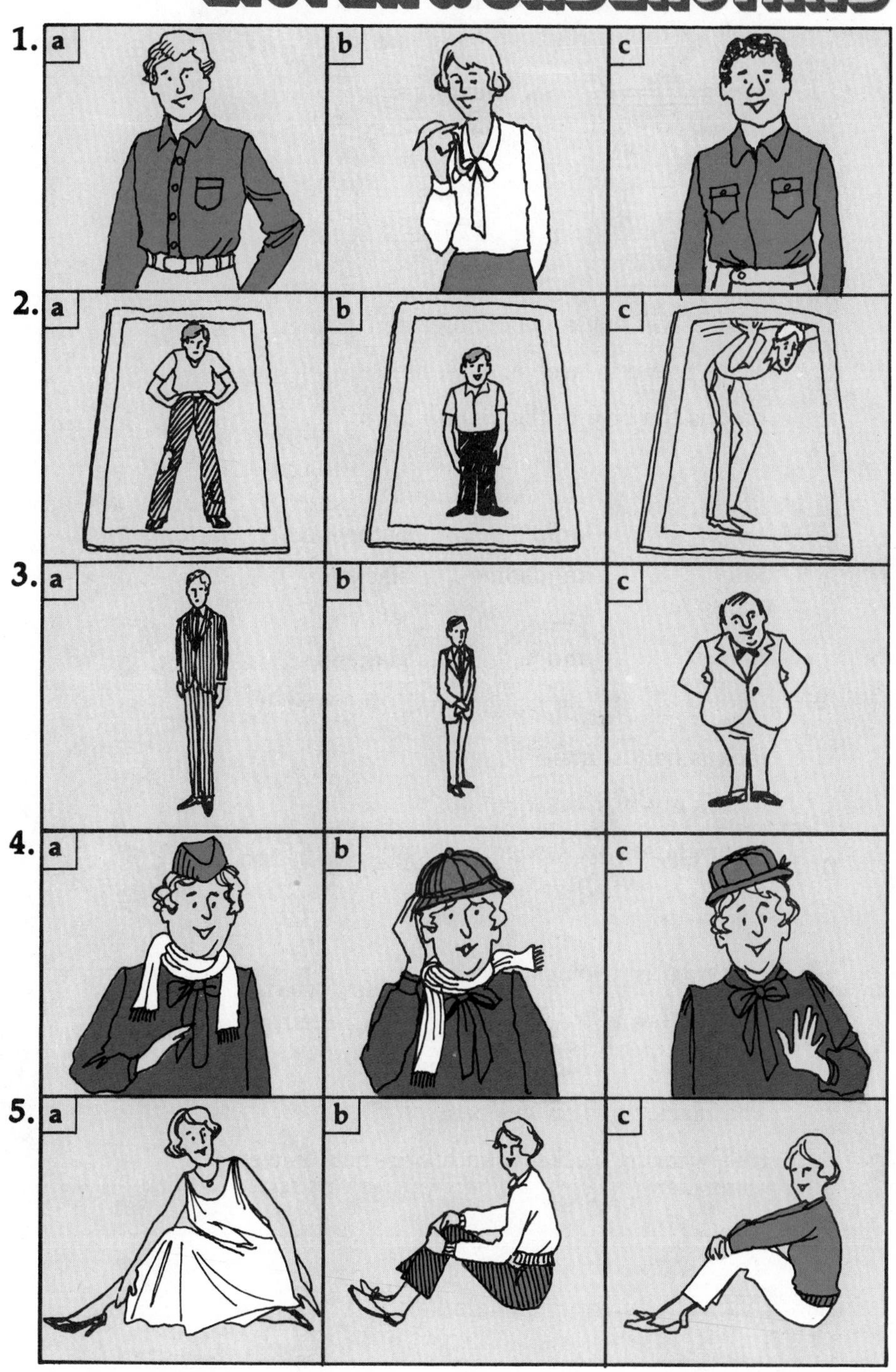

PRONUNCIATION

I.

friend	next	yellow
yes	twelve	dress
red	ten	Ted
sweater	bed	Fred

Fred is wearing a yellow sweater.
Ted's friend is twelve.
Fred is the boy in the red sweater.

II.

hat	lamp	bathrobe	Jack
Sally	handsome	slacks	that
black	Pat	jacket	last
at	and	glasses	man

Jack is handsome.
That's my black hat.
Your glasses are under the lamp.

III. My sweater is black.
Her red hat is on the bed.
My friend is wearing a yellow hat.
The black tie is on the bed.
He's wearing slacks, a bathrobe, and a sweater!

STATEMENTS:
TO BE +
PREDICATE ADJECTIVE:

He is tall.	His hair is black.
She is chubby.	Her eyes are blue.
He is fifteen.	He's handsome.

INFORMATION QUESTIONS:

How old is he?	**Who's** that boy?
What's she like?	**Who's** this?

VOCABULARY/EXPRESSIONS

and	handsome	pretty
blond(e)	how old	short
boy	last (name)	tall
boyfriend	look	that
chubby	look at	there
eyes	man	thin
girl	new	very
girl friend	over there	woman
hair	pants	

numbers thirteen - twenty

TEST YOURSELF

I. Fill in with *in, on, at* or *under.*

1. Where is the sofa? — It's . . . the living room.
2. Where is the bed? — It's . . . the bedroom.
3. Where is the raincoat? — It's . . . the chair.
4. Where are the glasses? — They're . . . the table.
5. Where are the shoes? — They're . . . the floor.

6. Where's Don?

a) It's three o'clock.
b) At the bus stop.
c) At six o'clock.

7. What time is it?

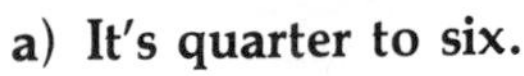

a) It's quarter to six.
b) At the bus stop.
c) At six o'clock.

8. When is the next bus?

a) It's three o'clock.
b) At the bus stop.
c) At half past six.

9. Who's Mary?

a) Her hair is blonde.
b) She is pretty.
c) She is the girl in the red dress.

10. **a) Who's Mary?**
    b) What's Mary?
    c) Where's Mary?

She is behind Mr. Shale.

II. 1. Who's this? . . . .

2. How old is he? . . . .

3. What color is his hair? . . . .

4. Is he chubby or thin? . . . .

5. What color are his eyes? . . . .

20

Bill

6. . . . . ? It's Ann.

7. . . . . ? It's Taylor.

8. . . . . ? She's fifteen.

9. . . . . ? They're brown.

10. . . . . ? It's red.

11. . . . . ? She's tall.

III.

Mr. Price Mr. Taylor Mr. King Mr. Novak

1. Where's Mr. Novak? He's . . . . Mr. King.

2. Where's Mr. Taylor? He's . . . . Mr. King.

3. Where's Mr. Price? He's . . . . Mr. Taylor.

4. Where's Mr. King? He's . . . . Mr. Taylor.

UNIT 5 FIVE

—Hi, dear.
What's Peter doing?
—He's drinking tea
in the living room.

—What's Mary doing?
—She's buying eggs at the store.

—And the dog?
—He's eating your newspaper.

Yes.

Do you like apples?

No.

1. Do you like carrots?

2. Do you like nuts?

3. Do you like grapes?

4. Do you like pears?

5. Do you like candy bars?

6. Do you like beans?

7. Do you like oranges?

8. Do you like peaches?

9. Do you like sandwiches?

What's she buying?
She's buying eggs.
What's she buying?
She's buying carrots.
What's she buying?
She's buying pears.

What's she buying now?

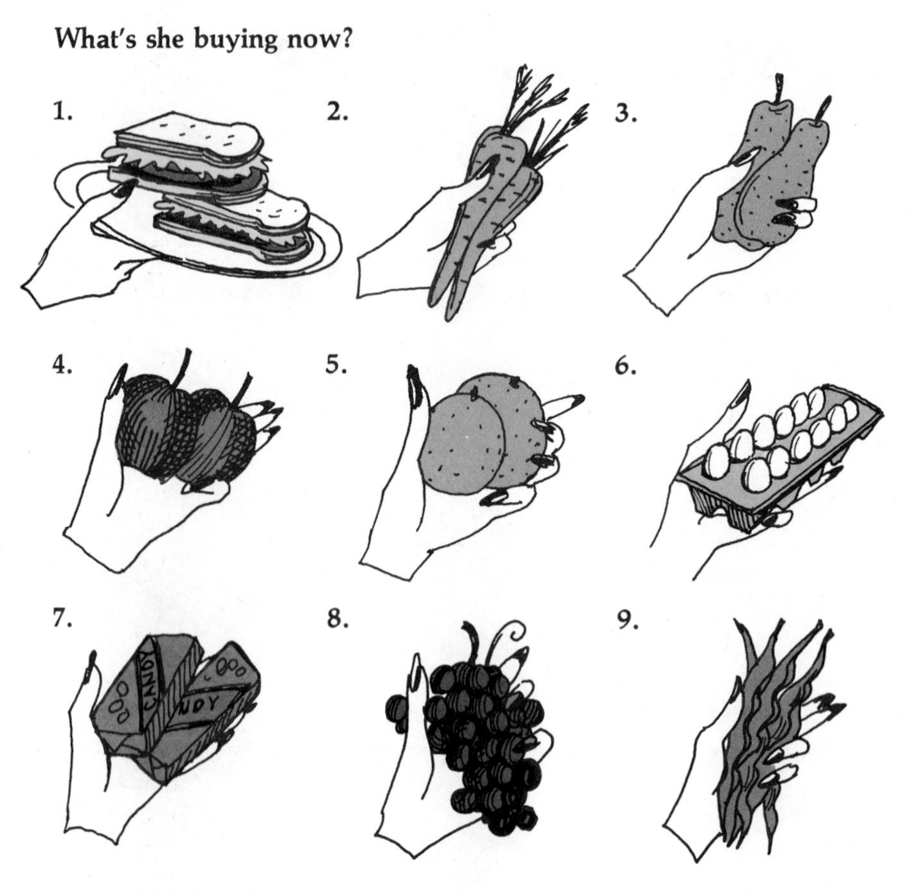

What's he eating?

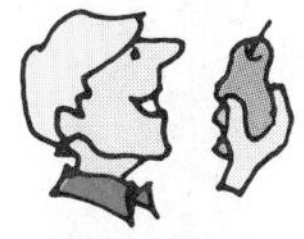

1. He's eating a pear.

2. He's eating a banana.

3. He's eating a candy bar.

4. He's eating an apple.

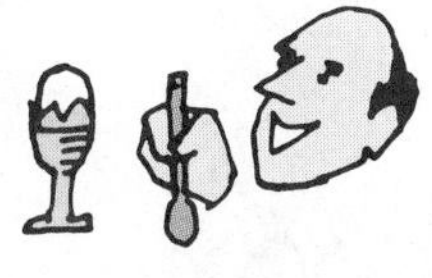

5. He's eating an egg.

6. He's eating an orange.

What's he eating now?

1.

2.

3.

4.

5.

6.

She's buying a banana.

She's buying an apple.

She's buying eggs.

What's she buying?

What's he drinking?  **He's drinking coffee.**

1. What's she drinking?  She's drinking water.

2. What's she drinking?  She's drinking lemonade.

3. What's he drinking?  He's drinking tea.

What's she eating?  **She's eating bread.**

1. What's he eating?  He's eating ice cream.

2. What's he eating?  He's eating meat.

3. What's she eating?  She's eating cheese.

1. What's he doing? He's drinking.

What's he drinking? He's drinking milk.

2. What's she doing? She's eating.

What's she eating? She's eating fish.

What's s(he) doing?

1.

2.

3.

4.

IN THE STORE

Dick is in the store.
Carol is in the store.
Mrs. Hill is in the store.
She is the owner.

MRS. HILL: Hello, Dick.
DICK: Hello, Mrs. Hill.
This is my friend, Carol.
MRS. HILL: Hello, Carol.
Pleased to meet you.
CAROL: Hello, Mrs. Hill.
Nice to meet *you.*
MRS. HILL: Can I help you?
DICK: Eight candy bars, please.
MRS. HILL: Here you are.
Anything else?
CAROL: Yes, six
sandwiches, please.
MRS. HILL: Is that all?
DICK: Yes, thanks,
How much is that?
MRS. HILL: That's four dollars, please.
CAROL: Here you are.
Thank you.

Where's he sitting?

He's sitting on a chair.

Where's she sitting?

She's sitting in an armchair.

1. on a stool

2. in a bathtub

3. in a car

4. on a sofa

What's he doing?

He's sitting in an armchair.

1.

2.

3.

4.

What's she reading?

She's reading a book.

1. a letter

2. a comic book

3. a newspaper

Dick is in his room.
He's sitting on the bed.
He's eating an apple.
He's drinking milk.
He's reading a book.

Mary is in her room.
She's sitting on the rug.
She's eating a pear.
She's drinking lemonade.
She's reading a comic book.

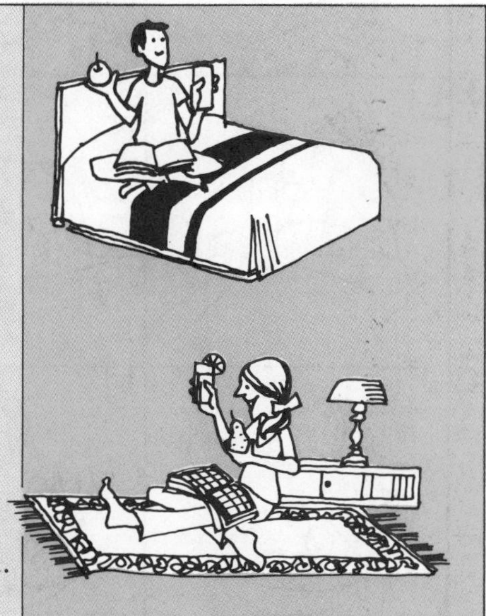

And Don?

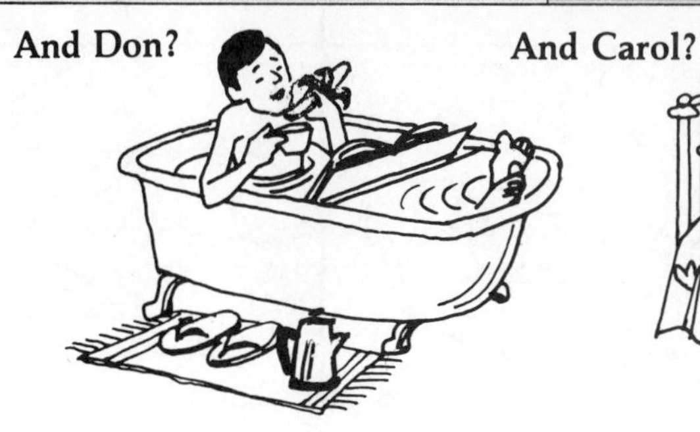

And Carol?

LISTEN & UNDERSTAND

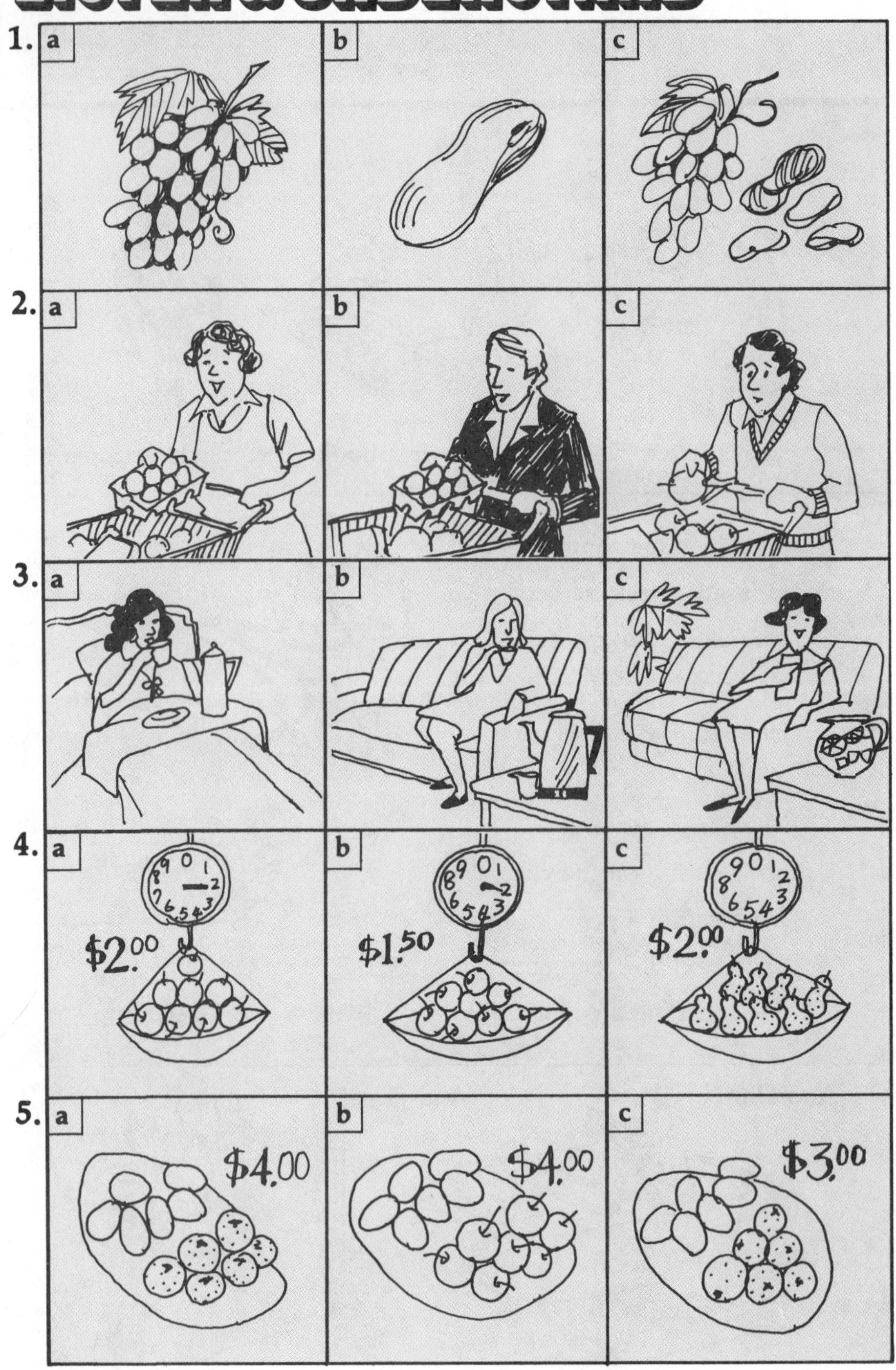

BASICS

THE PRESENT PROGRESSIVE:

What is he doing?

He	is buying	a banana.
	is eating	bread.
	is drinking	coffee.
	is reading	a book.
	is sitting	in an armchair.

USE OF ARTICLES:

He's eating **a** pear.	He's eating pears.
He's eating **an** apple.	He's eating apples.
He's eating fish.	He's drinking tea.

PLURAL OF NOUNS:

one carrot	three carrot**s**
one egg	four egg**s**
one peach	five peach**es**

VOCABULARY/EXPRESSIONS

an
apple(s)
armchair
banana(s)
bathtub
beans
book
bread
buying
candy bar(s)
car
carrot(s)
cheese
coffee
comic book
do
dog
doing
dollars
drinking
eating
egg(s)
fifty
fish
forty
grapes
ice cream
lemonade
letter
like
meat
milk
newspaper
nuts
orange(s)
owner
peaches
pear(s)
please
reading
sandwich(es)
sitting
stool
store
tea
water

Anything else?
Can I help you?
Here you are.
Hi, dear.
How much is that?
Is that all?
Nice to meet you.
Thank you.
Thanks.

—Tom! Hello, how *are* you?
—Fine, Rita. How are *you*?
—Not bad. Are you still a student?
—No, I'm a teacher now. How about you?
—I'm a doctor now.

—Are you still **a secretary?**

—No, I'm **an executive** now.

1. flight attendant **pilot**

2. nurse **doctor**

3. taxi driver **lawyer**

4. engineer **architect**

5. accountant **army officer**

6. waiter **chef**

1. I'm Eduardo Jimenez. I'm Colombian. I'm twenty. I'm a football player.

2. I'm Rita Perez. I'm Mexican. I'm twenty-seven. I'm a nurse.

3. I'm Susie Wong. I'm American. I'm nineteen. I'm a student.

4. I'm Maria Muniz. I'm Brazilian. I'm twenty-five. I'm a teacher.

5. I'm Pierre Goulet. I'm Canadian. I'm twenty-four. I'm a pilot.

6. I'm Tomás Moreno. I'm Puerto Rican. I'm thirty-eight. I'm a doctor.

NAME	NATIONALITY	AGE	OCCUPATION
1. Eduardo Jimenez			
2. Rita Perez			
3. Susie Wong			
4. Maria Muniz			
5. Pierre Goulet			
6. Tomás Moreno			
7. (for *you*)			

1. Are you Colombian?	No, I'm not.
Are you Mexican?	No, I'm not.
Are you American?	Yes, I am.
2. Are you twenty-six?	No, I'm not.
Are you nineteen?	Yes, I am.
3. Are you a taxi driver?	No, I'm not.
Are you a student?	Yes, I am.
4. You're Nancy Novak!	That's right.

Mexican 28 accountant Juan Fernandez	American 26 chef Nak Choung	Colombian 24 nurse Gloria Caldo
Brazilian 27 doctor Dr. Blume	Colombian 24 teacher Philippo Testa	Mexican 28 secretary Marta Sanchez
American 19 taxi driver Mario Martini	Brazilian 27 army officer General Branco	Mexican 19 flight attendant Margarita Gonzalez
Colombian 20 architect Elena Silva	American 19 student Nancy Novak	Brazilian 20 waiter Reynaldo Castro

PASSPORT CONTROL

—Good morning.
—Good morning. What's your name, please?
—My name is **Pat Goldman.**
—Are you **American**?
—Yes, I am.
—How old are you?
—I'm **twenty-six.**
—And what's your **occupation**?
—I'm **a doctor.**
—How long are you staying?
—Two weeks.
—Thank you. That's all.
—Thank *you.* Good-bye.

NAME	NATIONALITY	AGE	OCCUPATION
1. Pat Goldman	American	26	doctor
2. Roberto Flores	Mexican	33	teacher
3. John Cooper	English	19	secretary
4. Maria Tiant	Puerto Rican	29	pilot
5. Miguel Pinto	Venezuelan	30	executive
6. Aki Hiroshi	Japanese	22	accountant

LISTEN & UNDERSTAND

PRONUNCIATION

I.

nuts	socks	skirts
boots	hats	slacks
grapes	books	shorts

What's Mary eating?
Nuts and carrots.

II.

candy bars	jeans	beans
eggs	pears	shoes
chairs	girls	beds

He's eating eggs.
She's wearing red shoes.

III.

oranges	peaches	sandwiches
blouses	buses	glasses

That girl is buying two new blouses.
I'm eating peaches and oranges.

IV. Who's this?
Sue's buying oranges, pears, nuts and apples.
She's wearing red socks and white shoes.

BASICS

STATEMENTS

TO BE + PREDICATE NOUN/ADJECTIVE:	I am Elena Silva.
	You are pretty.
	He is an accountant.
	She is nineteen.
	He is Mexican.
PRONOUNS YOU & I:	Are you Colombian?
	Yes, I am. No, I'm not.

VOCABULARY/EXPRESSIONS

accountant
age
am
architect
army officer
chef
doctor
engineer
executive
flight attendant
football player
for
how long . . . ?
lawyer
nationality
nurse
occupation
pilot
secretary
sixty
staying
still
student
taxi driver
teacher
waiter
weeks

Fine.
How are you?
How about you?
Not bad.
That's all.
That's right.

TEST YOURSELF

I.

1. Hello Jerry. How are you?
   a) I'm fine, thanks.
   b) No, I'm not, thanks.
   c) I'm eighteen, thanks.

2. How old are you?
   a) Yes, I am.
   b) I'm seventeen.
   c) No, I'm a student now.

3. What's Ann doing? She's **a) doing** / **b) drinking** / **c) eating** tea.

4. What's Janet doing? She's **a) sitting** / **b) eating** / **c) doing** meat.

5. What's Pat doing? She's **a) drinking** / **b) reading** / **c) doing** a letter.

6. What's Sally doing? She's **a) sitting** / **b) doing** / **c) buying** in the car.

7. Here you are. Anything else?
   a) No, I'm not, thank you.
   b) That's all, thank you.
   c) Very well, thank you.

II. What's she buying? She's buying:

a) apples
b) sandwiches
c) eggs
d) pears
e) candy bars
f) carrots
g) nuts
h) oranges
i) ice cream
j) peaches
k) grapes
l) bread
m) fish
n) meat
o) cheese

III. Fill in with *a* or *an* where needed.

1. What's she buying? She's buying . . . eggs.
2. What's he drinking? He's drinking . . . water.
3. What's she eating? She's eating . . . banana.
4. What's he eating? He's eating . . . apple.
5. What's his occupation? He's . . . accountant.
6. What's her occupation? She's . . . pilot.

IV.

Puerto Rican 32 pilot John	American 22 accountant Betty
Mexican 23 nurse Carmen	Canadian 26 doctor Tom

1. Is . . . . still a nurse? Yes, she is.
2. What's her nationality? She's . . . .
3. Is Tom a . . . . ? Yes, he is.
4. What's . . . . ? He's Canadian.
5. . . . . ? He's twenty-six.
6. Is Betty still an . . . . ? Yes, she is.
7. Is John still a chef? No, he isn't. He's a . . . . . . now.
8. . . . . ? He's Puerto Rican.

UNIT 7 SEVEN

—This is my family in 1918.
—Who's this?
—It's my grandmother.

THE JOHNSON FAMILY

The Parents

Patricia Johnson (Pat)
mother
wife
48

Thomas Johnson (Tom)
father
husband
45

The Children

Thomas Johnson, Jr. (Tommy)
son
brother
15

Susan Johnson (Susie)
daughter
sister
21

I'm Pat Johnson. I'm a housewife. My husband's name is Tom. He's a chef. I'm forty-eight years old. Tom is forty-five. Tommy is my son. He's fifteen. Susie is my daughter. She's twenty-one. Tommy is still a student. Susie is an accountant.

1. Who is Tommy's father?	Thomas Johnson is.
2. Who is Tommy's sister?	Susie is.
3. Who is Tom's wife?	Patricia Johnson is.
4. Who is Pat Johnson's son?	Tommy is.
5. Who is a housewife?	Pat is.
6. Who is a chef?	Tom is.
7. Who are the Johnson children?	Tommy and Susie are.
8. Who are Susie's parents?	Patricia and Thomas Johnson are.

1. —Are you eighteen?
   —No, I'm not.
   —Are you nineteen?
   —Yes, I am.

2. —Are you mother and daughter?
   —No, we're not.
   —Are you grandmother and granddaughter?
   —Yes, we are.

3. —Are you husband and wife?
   —No, we're not.
   —Are you brother and sister?
   —No, we're not.
   —Well, are you father and daughter?
   —Yes, we are.

4. —Are they brother and sister?
   —No, they're not.
   —Are they husband and wife?
   —No, they're not.
   —Are they mother and son?
   —Yes, they are.

5. —Are you father and son?
   —No, we're not.
   —Are you brothers?
   —No, we're not.
   —Are you friends?
   —Yes, we are.
   We're good friends.

6. —Are you the grandfather?
   —No, I'm not.
   —Are you the father?
   —No, I'm not.
   —Well, what *are* you?
   —I'm the grandson!

I'm handsome.
Joe is handsome, too.

We're handsome!
We are both handsome.

1. Betty is happy. I'm happy, too.
2. I'm tired. My sister is tired, too.
3. I'm twenty-one. Rita is twenty-one, too.
4. Lucy is funny. I'm funny, too.
5. I'm cold. Daniel is cold, too.
6. Don is thin. I'm thin, too.

You're handsome,
and so is your friend.

You're handsome!
You are both handsome.

1. You are beautiful, and so is your friend.
2. You are friendly, and so is your sister.
3. Your friend is angry, and so are you.
4. Susan is short, and so are you.
5. You are pretty, and so is your friend.
6. She is tall, and so are you.

Which **coat** is **Jack's**?

The **big** coat is.

1. **scarf/Maria's**  **old**
2. **dog/Mike's**  **friendly**
3. **hat/Betty's**  **new**
4. **baby/Gloria's**  **chubby**

1. Is Tom in the car? — No, he's not. He's *under* the car!

2. Is the cat on the bed?

No, it's not. It's on the *table!*

3. Are the children in the yard?

No, they're not. They're in the *bathtub!*

4. Is Peter in front of the chair?

No, he's not. He's *behind* the chair!

5. Is the girl under the sofa?

No, she's not. She's *on* the sofa!

6. Are you in the car?

No, I'm not. I'm in the *bedroom!*

7. Are you under the table?

No, we're not. We're *on* the table!

8. Is your grandmother behind the armchair?

No, she's not. She's *in* the armchair!

1. Which room is she in?
   Is she in the kitchen?
   What's she doing?

Yes, she is.
She's cooking.

2. Which room is he in?
   Is he in the bathroom?
   What's he doing?

Yes, he is.
He's reading a book.

3. Which room are you in?
   Are you in the living room?
   Where *are* you?
   What are you doing?

No, I'm not.
I'm in the bedroom.
I'm watching TV.

4. Which room is she in?
   Is she in the kitchen?
   Where *is* she?
   What's she doing?

No, she's not.
She's in the living room.
She's listening to records.

5. Are they in the bedroom?
   Where *are* they?
   What are they doing?

No, they're not.
They're in the kitchen.
They're eating.

The Johnson family is at home. Mr. Johnson is in the kitchen. He is cooking. Mrs. Johnson is in the living room. She is sitting in an armchair. She's reading a newspaper. Tommy and his friend, Ricky, are in the yard. They are washing the car. Susie and her friend, Carol, are in Susie's bedroom. They are listening to records.

1. Is Mr. Johnson in the living room? — No, he isn't. He's in the kitchen.

2. Is Mrs. Johnson in the kitchen? — No, she isn't. She's in the living room

3. Is Mrs. Johnson reading a book? — No, she isn't. She's reading a newspaper.

4. Are Tommy and Ricky in the kitchen? — No, they aren't. They're in the yard.

5. Are they washing the bus? — No, they aren't. They're washing the car.

6. Are Susie and Carol in the kitchen? — No, they aren't. They're in Susie's bedroom.

LISTEN & UNDERSTAND

1. Mr. Gianetto is
   a) in the kitchen.
   b) in the living room.
   c) in the bathroom.

2. Mr. Gianetto is
   a) reading.
   b) listening to records.
   c) cooking.

3. Mrs. Gianetto is
   a) in the bedroom.
   b) in the kitchen.
   c) in the living room.

4. Mrs. Gianetto is
   a) reading.
   b) washing.
   c) cooking.

5. The boys are
   a) in the yard.
   b) in the kitchen.
   c) in the living room.

6. The boys are washing
   a) the dog.
   b) the car.
   c) the cat.

7. Susan is
   a) in her bedroom.
   b) in the bathroom.
   c) in the kitchen.

8. Susan is
   a) reading.
   b) eating.
   c) drinking.

9. The cat is
   a) under a chair in the living room.
   b) under a chair in the kitchen.
   c) on a chair in the living room.

INFORMATION QUESTIONS:

Who is Tommy's father?

Which coat is Jack's?

PERSONAL PRONOUNS:

I	am	eighteen.
He		chubby.
She	is	handsome.
It		at home.
We		
You	are	friends.
They		

POSSESSIVE OF NOUNS:

's

Tommy is Susie's brother.

Mr. and Mrs. Johnson are Tommy's parents.

NEGATIVE CONTRACTIONS:

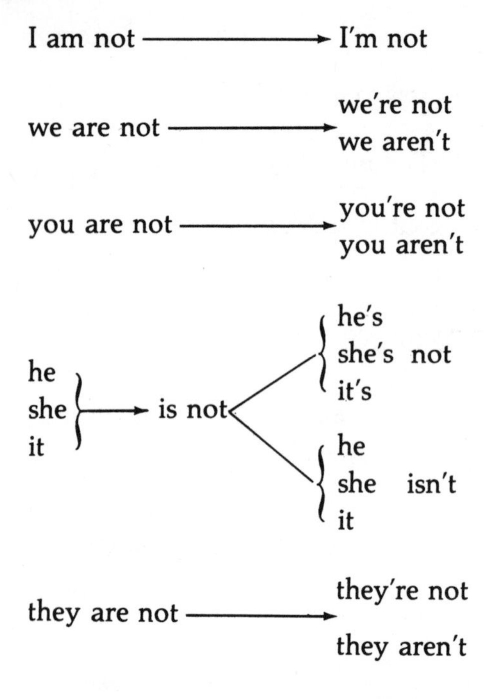

VOCABULARY/EXPRESSIONS

angry
baby
bathroom
beautiful
big
both
brother(s)
cat
children
coat
cold
cooking
daughter
family
father
friendly
funny
granddaughter
grandfather
grandmother
happy
housewife
husband
kitchen
listening to
mother
parents
records
seventy
sister
so
son
tired
too
TV
washing
watching
we
which
wife
wrong
yard
years (old)
at home

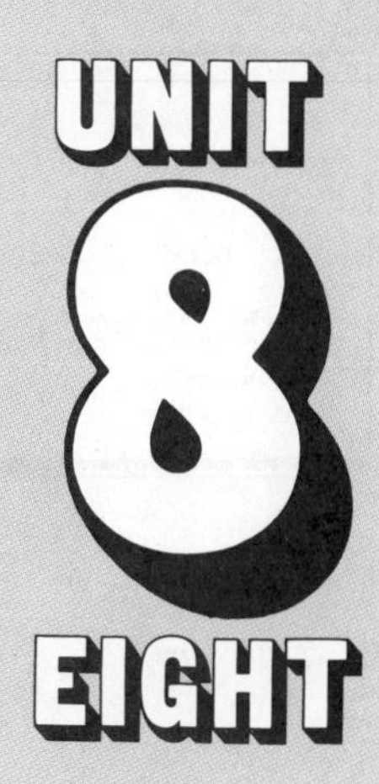

—Come on over, Gloria.
All our friends are here.
—Is Joe there?
—Yes, he is. He's playing the guitar.
—Are Tom and Betty there?
—Yes, they are. They're dancing.
—Is Nancy there?
—Yes, she is. She's singing.
—Is David there?
—Yes, he is. He's waiting for you!

Where's Peter going?

He's going to the bank.

1. Where's she going?

She's going to the post office.

2. Where are you going?

I'm going to the supermarket.

3. Where are you going?

We're going to the train station.

4. Where are they going?

They're going to the bus station.

5. Where are they going?

They're going to the police station.

6. Where's it going?

It's going to the airport.

7. Where's he going?

He's going to the theater.

8. Where's she going?

She's going to the library.

9. Where are they going?

They're going to the garage.

What's he doing?

He's singing.

1. What's she doing?

She's driving.

2. What's he doing?

He's sleeping.

3. What are they doing?

They're dancing.

4. What are they doing?

They're playing American football.

5. What are they doing?

They're watching TV.

—Hello.
—Hello, is this Tom?
—Yes, it is.
—Hi, Tom. This is Juan.
How are you?
—Fine, how are *you?*
—Fine, thanks. What are you doing?
—Ben is here. We're **watching TV.**
Come on over.

1. reading

2. listening to records

3. drinking coffee

4. playing the guitar

5. eating sandwiches

6. listening to the radio

How many tables are there? **There is one table.**
How many lamps are there? **There are two lamps.**

1. How many boys are there? There are three boys.
2. How many guitars are there? There are three guitars.
3. How many radios are there? There is one radio.
4. How many lamps are there? There are two lamps.
5. How many rugs are there? There is one rug.
6. How many records are there? There are four records.
7. How many chairs are there? There are two chairs.
8. How many tables are there? There is one table.

—Is there one **bank**,
or are there two **banks** here?
—There are two **banks**.

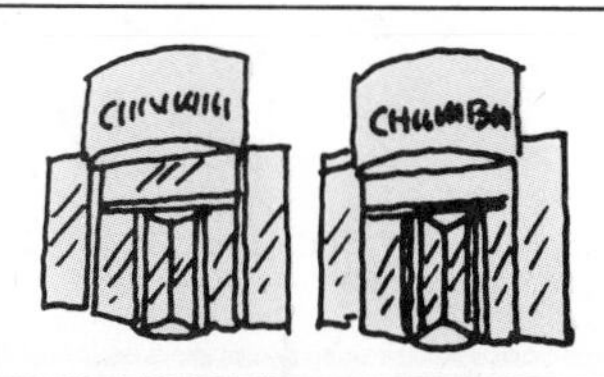

1. **supermarket**

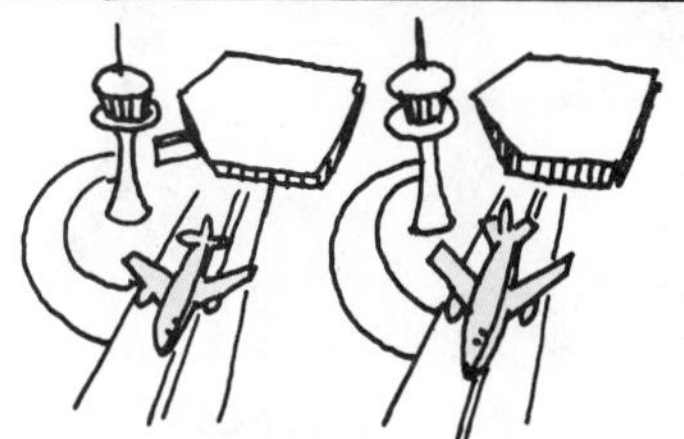

2. **airport**

3. **hotel**

4. **theater**

—Is there one **library**,
or are there two **libraries** here?
—There are two **libraries**.

1. **cemetery (cemeteries)**

2. **baby (babies)**

3. **strawberry (strawberries)**

4. **country (countries)**

—Is there one **garage**,
or are there two **garages** here?
—There are two **garages**.

1. **church (churches)**

2. **sandwich (sandwiches)**

2. **bridge (bridges)**

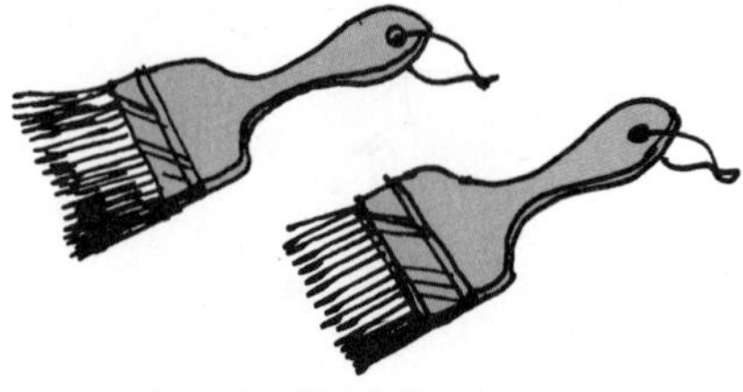

4. **brush (brushes)**

—Is there one **man**,
or are there two **men** here?
—There are two **men**.

1. **woman (women)**

2. **child (children)**

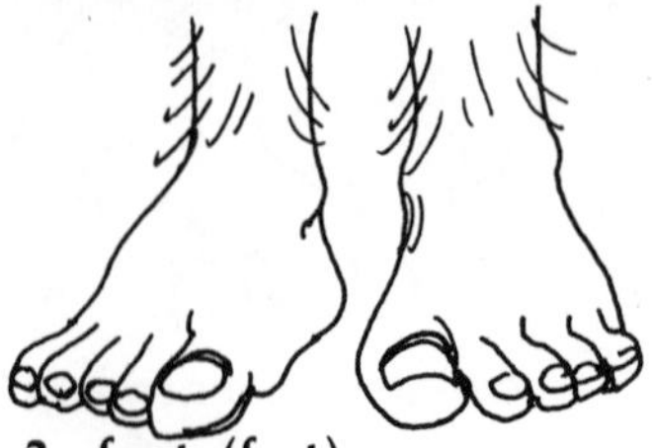

3. **foot (feet)**

4. **tooth (teeth)**

—What are you doing?
—I'm **reading a book.**

1.
2.
3.
4.
5.
6.
7.
8.
9.

Greenfield is a small village in England. It's not far from Manchester. There are five buses to Manchester every day, but there is only one train. There aren't many people on the train at six o'clock in the morning.

The church is in the middle of the village on the square. There are many other buildings on the square. There is a bank, the post office, the bus station and the police station. The library is behind the police station.

There are two garages in front of the bridge. There is a small cemetery behind the church. It's a small village, isn't it? There is no traffic, no noise, and no pollution.

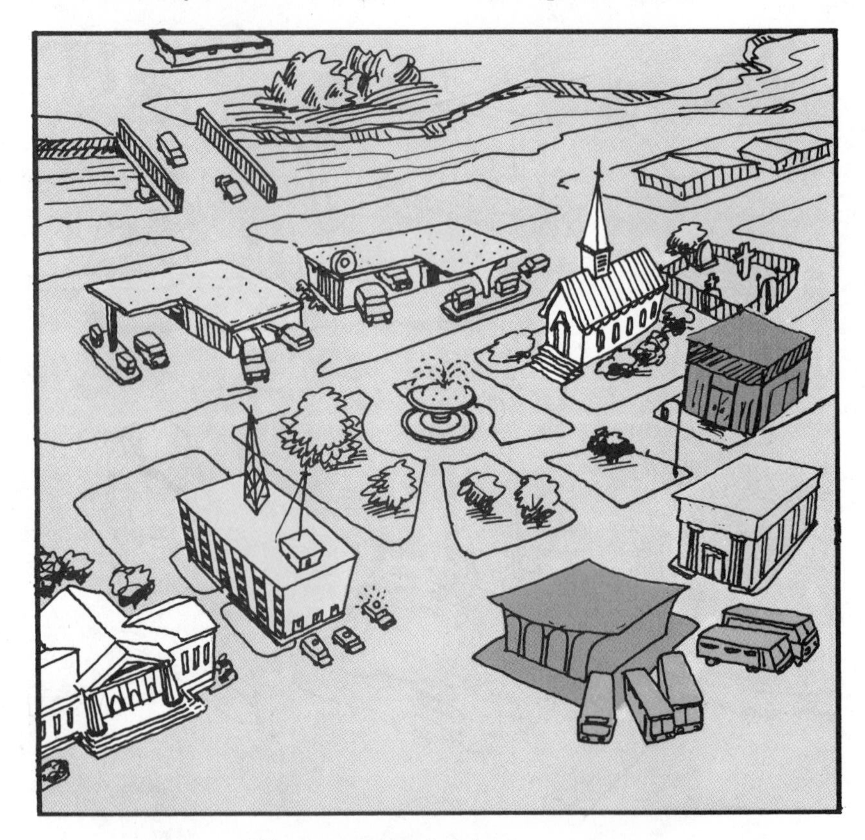

1. Where is Greenfield?
2. How many buses are there to Manchester?
3. Are there many people on the train?
4. What is in the middle of the village?
5. What other buildings are on the square?
6. Where's the library?
7. What are there in front of the bridge?
8. What's behind the church?

Boston is a small city, but there are many squares in it. This is Copley Square. The big Boston Public Library is on one side. There is an old church across from the library. There is a bus stop in front of the library.

There is a tall office building behind the library. You can see all of Boston from there. There are other buildings around the square. Some are old; some are new. It's a pretty square, isn't it? But there is a lot of traffic and a lot of noise in Boston. There is pollution, too.

1. Now ask and answer questions about Boston and Copley Square.

2. What about *your* city? What's it like?

LISTEN & UNDERSTAND

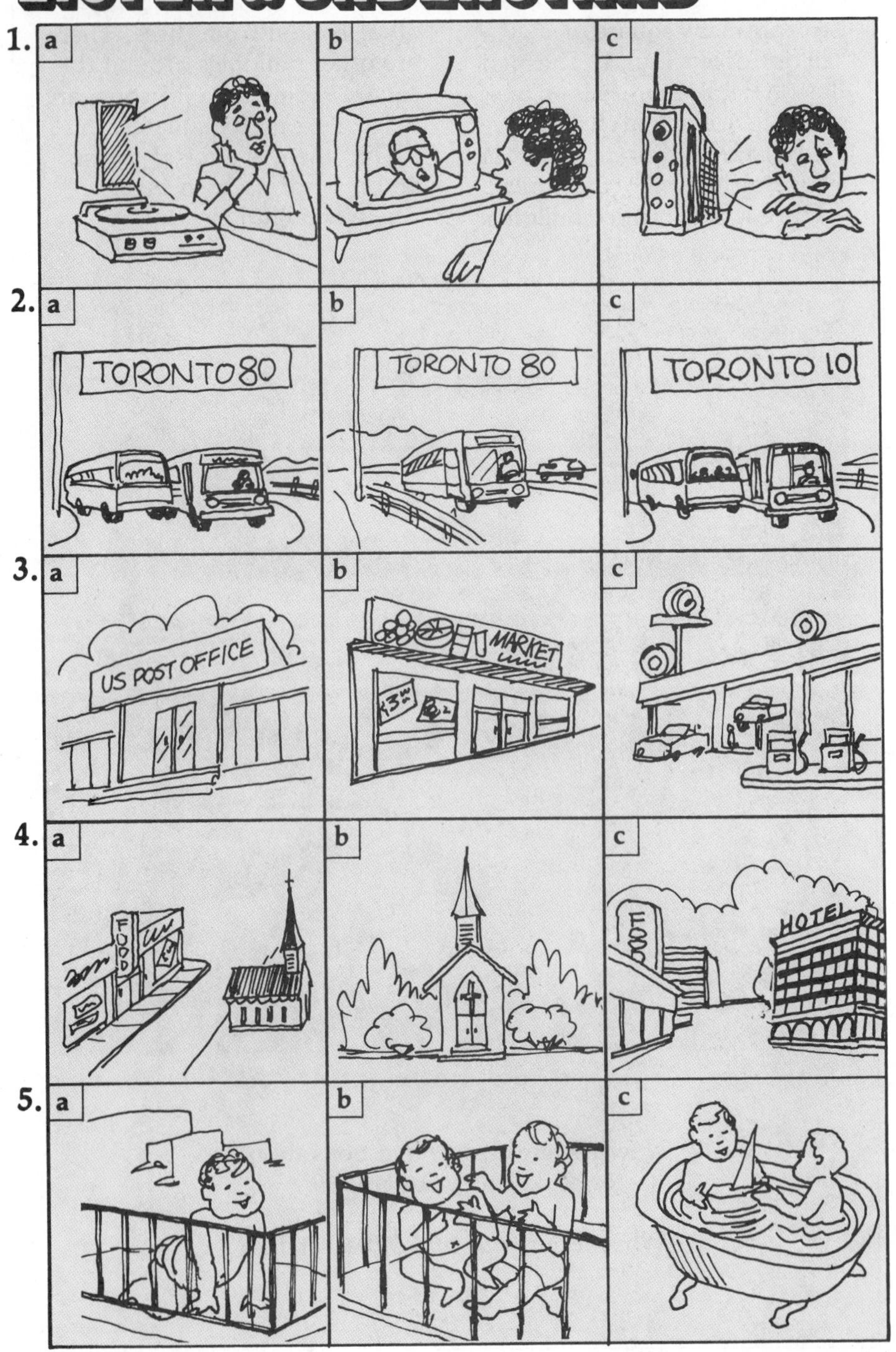

PRONUNCIATION

I.

she	tea	see
green	cheese	eating
meat	please	peach
Peter	teacher	three

She's reading.

Peter's eating a green peach.

II.

six	fish	sitting
milk	drinking	in
it	is	Bill
still	English	Tim

Is Bill drinking milk?

Tim is sitting in the living room.

III.

banks	guitars	blouses
airports	records	brushes
hats	schools	watches
weeks	hotels	offices
bus	trees	churches
across	flowers	bridges

BASICS

INFORMATION QUESTIONS:

Where's he going?
How many lamps are there?

STATEMENTS:

There is one train station.
There are two bus stations.

NOUN PLURALS:

bank	bus	country	church
banks	buses	countries	churches
child	foot	man	woman
children	feet	men	women

VOCABULARY/EXPRESSIONS

across from
airport(s)
a lot of
all
around
babies
bank(s)
bridge(s)
brush(es)
buildings
bus station(s)
but
cemetery(ies)
child
church(es)
city
country(ies)
dancing
day
driving
eighty
every
far
feet
foot
from
garage(s)
going
guitar(s)
here
hotel(s)
how many
in the middle of
library(ies)
men
noise
of
office
only
other
our
people
playing
police station
pollution
post office
radio(s)
side
singing
sleeping
small
some
square(s)
strawberry(ies)
supermarket(s)
teeth
theater(s)
to
tooth
traffic
train
train station
village
waiting for
women

Come on over.

TEST YOURSELF

I. Fill in with *is, am,* or *are.*

1. They . . . pretty.
2. I . . . a student.
3. You . . . handsome.
4. The apples . . . on the table.
5. **a) He** / **b) I** / **c) They** is in the kitchen.
6. **a) She** / **b) I** / **c) They** are children.

II.

Mr. Riley (Paul)

Mrs. Riley (Judy)

Conor Riley

Anne Riley

1. Who is Judy's **a) son? b) daughter? c) wife?** Conor is.
2. Who is Paul's **a) son? b) daughter? c) wife?** Anne is.
3. Who is Paul's **a) mother? b) wife? c) husband?** Judy is.
4. Who is Conor's **a) sister? b) brother? c) family?** Anne is.
5. Who are Conor's **a) parents? b) children? c) friends?** Paul and Judy are.

III. How many are there?

Begin your answers with *there is* or *there are.*

1. **2.**  **3.**

4.  **5.**

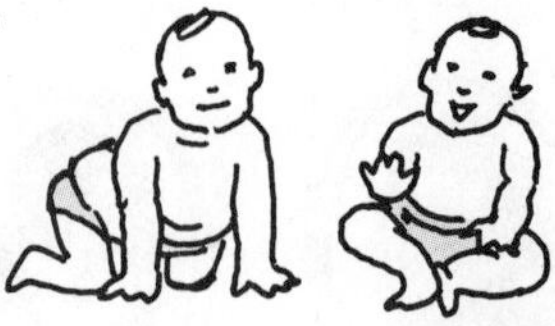

6.  **7.**  **8.**

IV.

1. What's John doing? He's **a) eating.** **b) playing the guitar.** **c) sleeping.**

2. What's Mary doing? She's **a) drinking.** **b) listening to records.** **c) singing.**

3. What's Sam doing? He's **a) eating.** **b) singing.** **c) sleeping.**

4. What's Helen doing? She's **a) washing.** **b) sleeping.** **c) dancing.**

V. 1. What . . . .? — They're watching TV.

2. Where . . . .? — We're going to the library.

3. How . . . . .there? — There are two babies.

4. Is there one man, or are there . . . . here? — There are two . . . .

5. Is there one woman there? — No, there are two . . . .

6. Is there one library in Millville? — No, there are four . . . .

7. My friend is tall and so are you. — Yes, ...

8. Your brother is handsome, and . . . . I. — Yes, ...

VI. 1. Where's the bus going? . . . .

2. Where's Frank going? . . . .

3. Where's Beth going? . . . .

4. Where's Henry going? . . . .

VII. 1. Am I handsome? — No, ...

2. Are you twenty? — No, ...

3. Is Alice twenty? — No, ...

4. Are they brother and sister? — No, ...

UNIT 9 NINE

—Whose cup is this?
—It's Mary's.
—Well, give it to her.

—Whose glasses are these?
—They're Juan's.
—Well, give them to him.

1. *This* racket is old, but *that* racket is new.

2. *This* is a Canadian player, and *that* is a Mexican player.

3. *These* roller skates are Peter's, and *those* ice skates are Mary's.

4. *These* circles are big, but *those* squares are small.

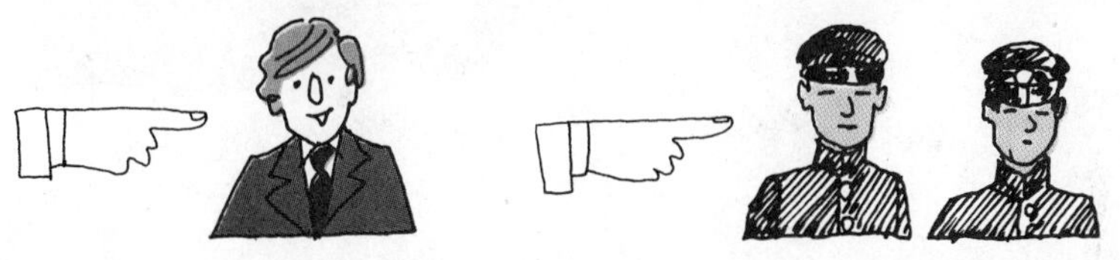

1. This is an English student.

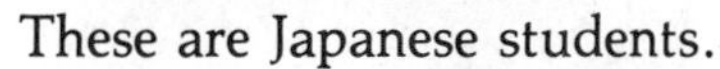

These are Japanese students.

2. That is a Turkish pilot.

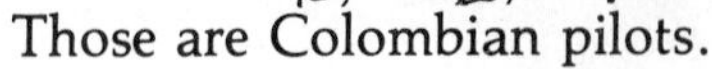

Those are Colombian pilots.

3. These are American footballs. Those are Brazilian footballs.

What are they saying? Use **this, that, these** *or* **those** *in your answers.*

—Is this **Mr. Green's** office?
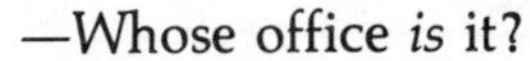
—Whose office *is* it?

—No, it isn't.
—It's **Ms. Pott's.**

—Is this your **shirt?**
—Whose **shirt** *is* it?

—No, it isn't.
—It's **Tom Marks's.**

1. **sweater/Mike Jones's**
2. **hat/Betty Church's**
3. **tie/Dennis's**
4. **car/Maria March's**
5. **boyfriend/Sally Burns's**
6. **racket/James's**

—Is this your **rug?**
—Whose **rug** *is* it?

—No, it isn't.
—It's **the Greens'.**

1. **bedroom/the boys'**
2. **teacher/the girls'**
3. **car/the Blacks'**
4. **football/the students'**
5. **store/the Johnsons'**
6. **garage/the Kings'**

THE COSTUME PARTY

What's Dick wearing?

1. Bess's hat
2. . . . .
3. . . . .
4. Mary's blouse
5. Bess's skirt
6. Fred's pants
7. . . . .
8. Betty's shoes

What's Mike wearing?

1. . . . .
2. . . . .
3. . . . .
4. . . . .
5. . . . .
6. . . . .
7. . . . .
8. . . . .

I	am		me.
He She	is		him. her.
		tired, so Jack's helping	
We You They	are		us. you. them.

	my		me.
	his		him.
That's	her	book, so give it to	her.
	our		us.
	their		them.

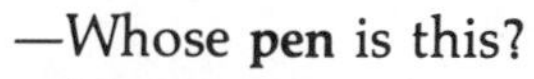
—Whose **pen** is this?
—It's **Tom's.**
—Well, give it to **him.**

1. **2.** **3.**

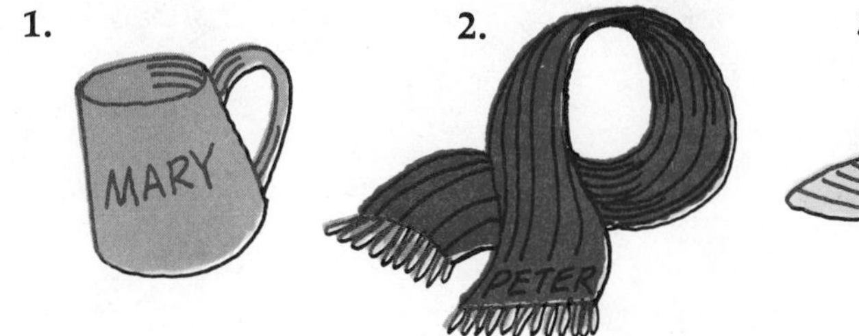

Who's this?
It's Tom.

What's this?
It's a book.
Whose is it?
It's Tom's.

What's **Tom** doing?
He's reading.

1. Mary

2. James

3. Lucy

4. Mr. Dodds

5. Bess

LISTEN & UNDERSTAND

BASICS

POSSESSIVE OF NOUNS:

Whose shirt is this? It's **the Browns'.** / **the boys'.** / **Jack's.** / **Bess's.**

OBJECT PRONOUNS:

Give the book to **me.**

Tom is helping **me.** / **you.** / **him.** / **her.** / **us.** / **them.**

DEMONSTRATIVE ADJECTIVES/PRONOUNS:

this car

that car

these cars
These are cars.

those cars
Those are cars.

POSSESSIVE ADJECTIVES:

Our / **Your** / **Their** dog is very big.

VOCABULARY/EXPRESSIONS

circles	ice skates	their
costume party	me	them
cup	ninety	these
give	office	those
gloves	pen	us
helping	racket	whose
her	roller skates	
him	so	

UNIT
10
TEN
1.
Hurry!
2.
Where are you going?
To New York.
Hurry!
3.
When are you going?
At ten
o'clock!
4.
It's quarter to ten now.
Yes, it's late.
Hurry!

1. What time is it?

It's ten-fifteen.

2. What time is it?

It's ten-thirty.

3. What time is it?

It's ten-twenty.

4. What time is it?

It's ten forty-five.

—Hurry, it's late.
—What time is it?
—It's **ten-twenty.**
—No, it isn't. It's only **nine-thirty**. It's early.

1.

2.

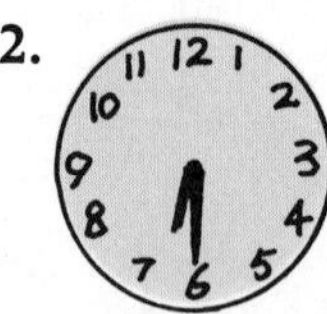

3.

4.

1. When are you going? 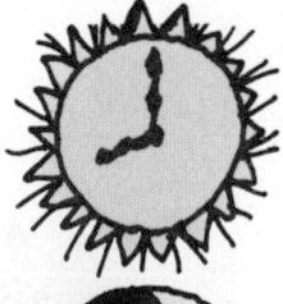 In the morning.

2. When are you going?  In the evening.

3. When are you going?  In the afternoon.

4. When are you going?  At noon.

5. When are you going?  At midnight.

6. When are you going?  At night.

—Good afternoon.
—Good afternoon, sir.
—When is your next flight to Mexico?
—Tomorrow at **seven**.
—Seven **in the morning,** or seven **in the evening?**
—**In the evening.** It's flight 602.
—Thank you.
—Thank you, sir. Good-bye.

1.	**9:00**	**morning/night**
2.	**12:00**	**noon/midnight**
3.	**5:00**	**morning/afternoon**

—Where are you going?
—I'm going to London.
—Who's going with you?
—My mother is.
—When are you going?
—At ten o'clock.

1. Rio	my cousin	8:15
2. New York City	my grandfather	9:20
3. Montreal	my grandmother	10:45
4. Mexico City	my aunt	3:30
5. Los Angeles	my uncle	5:45

—What are you doing tonight?
—I'm going to a party.
—What are you wearing?
—I'm wearing my new blouse,
my red skirt, and
my black boots.
—When are you going?
—At seven-thirty.

1. tonight
   a dance
   blue dress, yellow scarf
   8:00

2. today
   the movies
   old jeans, white sweater
   4:30

3. this morning
   church
   brown coat, red hat
   6:30

4. this afternoon
   the football game
   yellow suit, brown shoes
   2:15

5. tomorrow night
   a concert
   black dress, white coat
   7:30

6. Saturday night
   the museum
   new slacks, gray blouse,
   green jacket
   8:15

LISTEN & UNDERSTAND

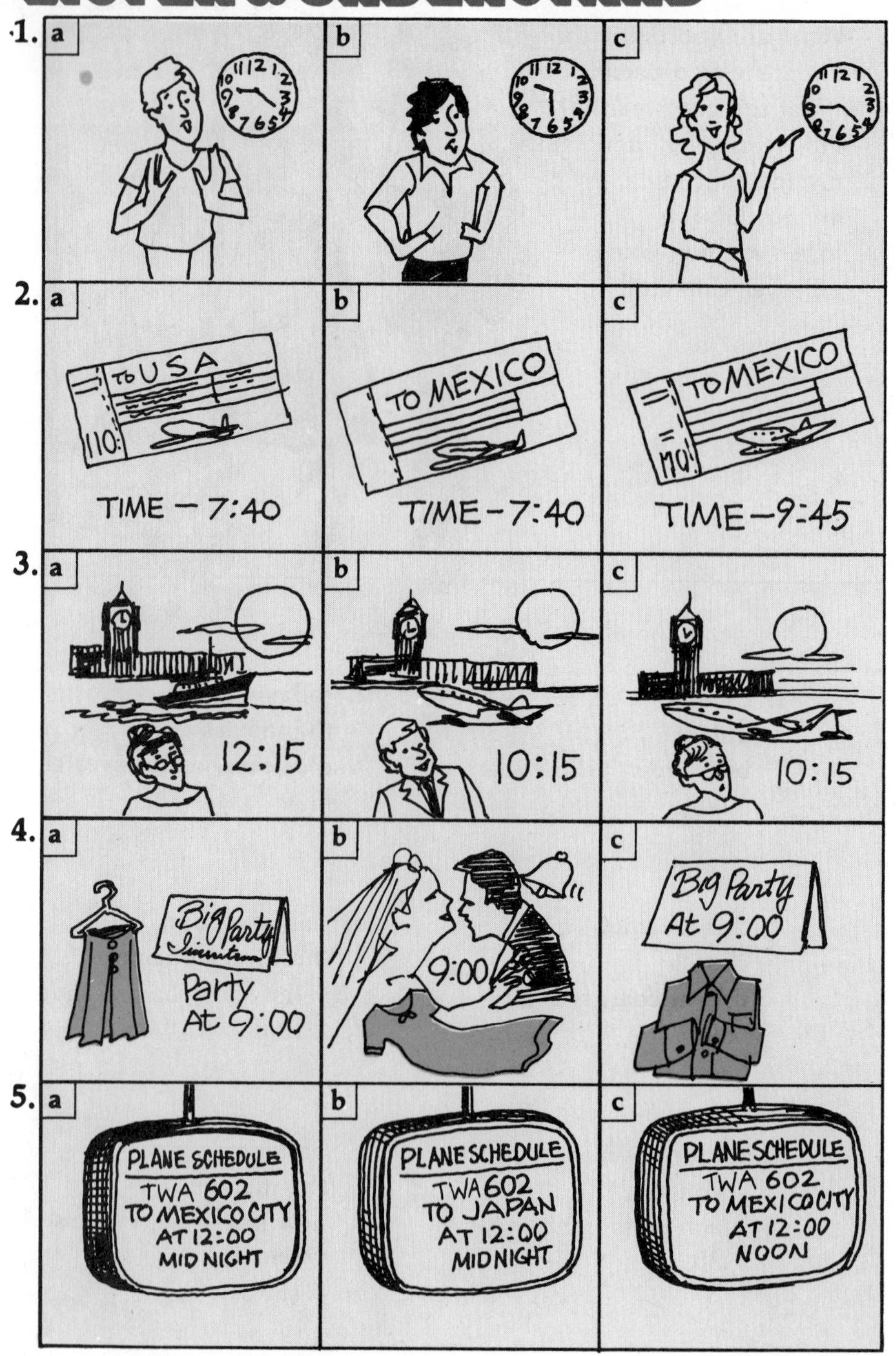

PRONUNCIATION

I.	tall	teacher	ten	suit
	to	eight	tonight	meat
	cemetery	water	stop	pilot

Our teacher is tall.

We're going tonight at ten to eight.

II.	building	side	around	bedroom
	dancing	daughter	drinking	old
	dress	child	lemonade	blonde

Her daughter is drinking lemonade.

Don is very handsome.

III.	thin	theater	three
	thirty	both	thanks

Bill and Sam are both thin.

We're going to the theater at three-thirty.

IV.	that	these	other
	father	there	brother
	mother	they	them

That's my brother over there.

My mother's father is my grandfather.

V. That's Tom's lemonade.

My father is a teacher.

Tom's going to the theater with his brother tonight.

They are both drinking tea.

They're going to London at two-thirty.

BASICS

TIME PHRASES:

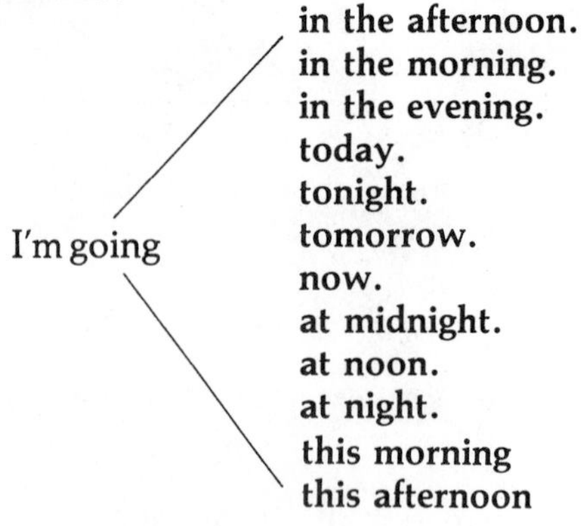

I'm going
in the afternoon.
in the morning.
in the evening.
today.
tonight.
tomorrow.
now.
at midnight.
at noon.
at night.
this morning
this afternoon

TIME STRUCTURES:

It's ten-twenty (10:20).

It's ten-thirty (10:30).

QUESTION WORDS:

Where are you going? **To London.**

When are you going? **At ten o'clock in the morning.**

Who's going with you? **John is.**

VOCABULARY/EXPRESSIONS

afternoon
aunt
concert
cousin
dance
evening
flight
football game
movies

museum
night
one hundred
sir
today
tomorrow
tonight
uncle
with

Good afternoon.
Hurry!
It's late (early).

TEST YOURSELF

I.

1. I'm tired, so Frank's helping **a) them.** **b) me.** **c) us.**

2. We're tired, so Frank's helping **a) us.** **b) me.** **c) you.**

3. They're tired, so Frank's helping **a) her.** **b) them.** **c) him.**

4. That's **a) their** **b) our** **c) her** book, so give it to them.

5. This is **a) his** **b) her** **c) your** scarf. Give it to him.

II. Fill in with *this, that, these* or *those.*

1. Look at . . .skates over there.
2. Is . . .your mother across the street?
3. Who are . . .players over there?
4. Aren't . . .shoes in that store pretty?
5. Here you are. . . .is your ice cream.
6. . . . grapes on that table are good, too.
7. Are . . .glasses here Tom's?
8. . . . are my boots;. . . are your boots under the table.

III.

1. .... hat is that? — It's John's.

2. .... shoes are these? — .... Sally's.

3. These books are Mike Jones's. — Well, give ....

4. This is your pen. — Well, give ....

5. ....? — I'm going to London.

6. .... to London? — Tomorrow.

7. .... going with your sister? — No, I'm not.

8. .... ? — My brother is.

9. What time is it? — It's ....

10. What time is it? — It's ....

11. What time is it?  1:30 — It's ....

12. What time is it?  2:40 — It's ....

UNIT 11 ELEVEN

—Can you type?
—No, I can't.

—Can you take shorthand?
—No, I can't.

—Can you make coffee?
—Yes, I can.
—Good. You're hired.

Can Sally skate?		**No, she can't.**

1. Can Sam type?  No, he can't.

2. Can they ski?  Yes, they can.

3. Can they run?  Yes, they can.

4. Can it sing?  Yes, it can.

5. Can it sing?  No, it can't.

6. Can you walk?  No, we can't.

7. Can he drive?  No, he can't.

Can you help me?

No, I'm sorry.
I have to
wash the clothes.

1. Can Tommy help me?

No, I'm sorry.
He has to study.

2. Can Susan help me?

No, I'm sorry.
She has to
clean the windows.

3. Can Bill help me?

No, I'm sorry.
He has to
brush the dog.

4. Can Fred and Ron help me?

No, I'm sorry.
They have to
polish the car.

5. Well, I'm going to play tennis.

No, you can't.
You have to
help *me!*

—Mom, can I go to the **movies**?
—No, you can't. You have to do your homework.

1. tennis match **2. concert** **3. museum** **4. theater**

—Can you **skate**?
—No, I can't.

1.

2.

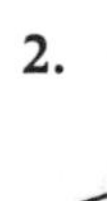

3.

4.

1. What sport can he play?

He can play soccer.

2. What sport can she play?

She can play baseball.

3. What sport can they play?

They can play tennis.

4. What sport can you play?

I can play table tennis.

—What game can he play?
—He can play **chess.**

1. backgammon

2. cards

3. checkers

4. Monopoly

1. What instrument can she play?

She can play the bass.

2. What instrument can he play?

He can play the drums.

3. What instrument can they play?

They can play the piano.

4. What instrument can you play?

I can play the flute.

—Can he **play baseball?**
—Yes, he's **playing baseball** now.

1. **skate**
2. **swim**
3. **play chess**
4. **type**
5. **play tennis**
6. **play the bass**

How about you? What can **you** *do?*

THE CONCERT

Jack is waiting for Gloria.
They're going to a rock concert.
The concert is at seven o'clock.
It's quarter to seven now.
But Gloria is late.
She's still at home.
She's washing her hair.

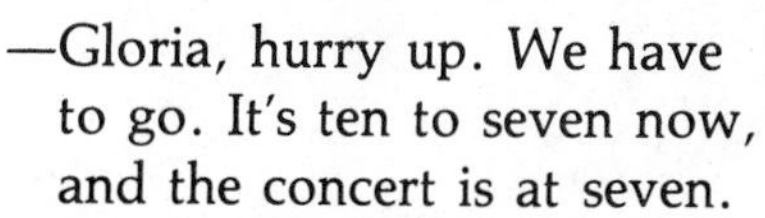

—Gloria, hurry up. We have
to go. It's ten to seven now,
and the concert is at seven.
—No, the concert is at eight.
Look in the newspaper.
—I *am* looking in the
newspaper. The concert is at
seven. Can't you read?
—Oh dear. I'm sorry. Well,
come in and wait.

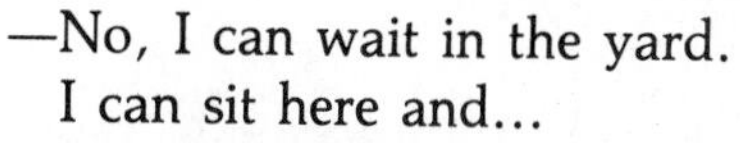

—No, I can wait in the yard.
I can sit here and...
—No! Stop! You can't sit...
—Oh yes I can.
—Oh Jack. Look at your pants.
Look at your hands!
Look at the sign! Can't *you*
read?
—Oh. Wet Paint.
Well, don't hurry, Gloria.
I have to go home and
change my suit.

LISTEN & UNDERSTAND

BASICS

CAN:

I can swim. He can skate.
Can you make coffee?
Mom, can I go to the movies?

TO HAVE TO:

I You They	have to	go. study. read this book.
He She	has to	

VOCABULARY/EXPRESSIONS

backgammon
baseball
bass
cards
change
checkers
chess
clean
clothes
drive
drums
flute
game
go
going to
hands
hired
homework
instrument
looking
make
Monopoly
piano
play
polish
read
rock concert
run
sign
sing
sit
skate
skating
ski
soccer
sport
study
swim
swimming
table tennis
tennis
tennis match
type
typing
wait
walk
wash
windows

Come in.
Good.
Hurry up!
Oh dear.
Stop!
take shorthand
wet paint

UNIT 12 TWELVE

—Hello, James. How are you?
—Terrible!
—What's the matter with you?
—I have a bad **tooth.**

—When are the **Smiths** coming for **dinner**?
—On **Sunday**.

1\.

2\.

3\.

4\.

5\.

6\.

—When are you taking your vacation this year?
—In **January**.
—Oh, do you like a **winter** vacation?
—Yes.

WINTER — January

S	M	T	W	T	F	S
	1	2	3	4	5	6
7	8	9	10	11	12	13
14	15	16	17	18	19	20
21	22	23	24	25	26	27
28	29	30	31			

WINTER — February

S	M	T	W	T	F	S
				1	2	3
4	5	6	7	8	9	10
11	12	13	14	15	16	17
18	19	20	21	22	23	24
25	26	27	28			

SPRING — March

S	M	T	W	T	F	S
				1	2	3
4	5	6	7	8	9	10
11	12	13	14	15	16	17
18	19	20	21	22	23	24
25	26	27	28	29	30	31

SPRING — April

S	M	T	W	T	F	S
1	2	3	4	5	6	7
8	9	10	11	12	13	14
15	16	17	18	19	20	21
22	23	24	25	26	27	28
29	30					

SPRING — May

S	M	T	W	T	F	S
		1	2	3	4	5
6	7	8	9	10	11	12
13	14	15	16	17	18	19
20	21	22	23	24	25	26
27	28	29	30	31		

SUMMER — June

S	M	T	W	T	F	S
					1	2
3	4	5	6	7	8	9
10	11	12	13	14	15	16
17	18	19	20	21	22	23
24	25	26	27	28	29	30

SUMMER — July

S	M	T	W	T	F	S
1	2	3	4	5	6	7
8	9	10	11	12	13	14
15	16	17	18	19	20	21
22	23	24	25	26	27	28
29	30	31				

SUMMER — August

S	M	T	W	T	F	S
			1	2	3	4
5	6	7	8	9	10	11
12	13	14	15	16	17	18
19	20	21	22	23	24	25
26	27	28	29	30	31	

FALL — September

S	M	T	W	T	F	S
						1
2	3	4	5	6	7	8
9	10	11	12	13	14	15
16	17	18	19	20	21	22
23	24	25	26	27	28	29
30						

FALL — October

S	M	T	W	T	F	S
	1	2	3	4	5	6
7	8	9	10	11	12	13
14	15	16	17	18	19	20
21	22	23	24	25	26	27
28	29	30	31			

FALL — November

S	M	T	W	T	F	S
				1	2	3
4	5	6	7	8	9	10
11	12	13	14	15	16	17
18	19	20	21	22	23	24
25	26	27	28	29	30	

WINTER — December

S	M	T	W	T	F	S
						1
2	3	4	5	6	7	8
9	10	11	12	13	14	15
16	17	18	19	20	21	22
23	24	25	26	27	28	29
30	31					

1. What's the weather like?

2. What's the weather like?

3. What's the weather like?

4. What's the weather like?

5. What's the weather like?

6. What's the weather like?

7. What's the weather like?

8. What's the weather like?

9. What's the weather like?

10. What's the weather like?

It's drizzling.

It's raining.

It's pouring.

It's snowing.

It's hot.

It's warm.

It's cold.

It's cloudy.

It's sunny.

It's windy.

—Hi, this is **John** in **San Francisco.**
—Hi, **John.**
When are you coming?
—I'm leaving here at **nine o'clock.**
What's the weather like there?
—It's hot and sunny here.
What's the weather like in
San Francisco?
—It's **raining.**
—Well, come and enjoy the sun.
—Right! See you soon.

—Hello, Tom. This is **Sue.**
—Hello, **Sue.** Where are you?
—I'm on vacation in **Florida.**
—What's the weather like?
—It's **hot.**

LISTEN & UNDERSTAND

INFORMATION QUESTIONS:

What's the matter with you?
What's the weather like?
When are they coming?

PREPOSITIONS OF TIME:

They're coming **on** Friday.
I'm going **in** December.
I'm eating **at** eight.

PREDICATE ADJECTIVES:

The weather is **sunny.**
It's **warm.**

DAYS OF THE WEEK

MONTHS OF THE YEAR

VOCABULARY/EXPRESSIONS

after
ankle
arm
bad
before
breakfast
chest
cloudy
come
dinner
drinks
drizzling
ear
elbow
enjoy
fall
finger
have
head
hip
hot
knee
leaving
leg
lunch
nose
pouring
raining
snowing
spring
stomach
summer
sun
sunny
taking
throat
thumb
toe
vacation
warm
weather
windy
winter
wrist
year

See you soon.
Terrible!
What's the matter with you?

GRAMMAR HIGHLIGHTS

PRONOUNS

PERSONAL PRONOUNS (Units 2, 6, 7)

I am eighteen.

He is chubby.
She is handsome.
It is at home.

We / **You** / **They** are friends.

OBJECT PRONOUNS (Unit 9)

Give the book to **me.**
Tom is helping **me/you/him/her/us/them.**

DEMONSTRATIVE PRONOUNS (Units 2, 9)

This is her hat.
These are cars.

That is his hat.
Those are cars.

ADJECTIVES

ADJECTIVE + NOUN (Unit 2)

Bill is wearing a **red** shirt.

I'm wearing my **new** blouse.

PREDICATE ADJECTIVES/WITH **both/so** (Units 4, 6, 7, 12)

The weather is **sunny**.

We are **tired**.

You're **handsome** and **so** is your friend.
You are **both handsome**.

POSSESSIVE ADJECTIVES (Units 1, 9)

This is **my** / **your** / **his** / **her** friend.

Our / **Your** / **Their** dog is very big.

DEMONSTRATIVE ADJECTIVES (Units 4, 9)

This car is red.
These cars are old.

That car is green.
Those cars are new.

PREPOSITIONS OF PLACE/TIME (Units 3, 12)

The tie	is	**on** / **under**	the chair.
Mr. Jones	is	**in front of** / **behind**	Mrs. Rivera.

Don is **at** the bus stop.
Lucy is **in** the bedroom.

They're coming **on** Friday. I'm going **in** May. I'm eating **at** eight.

CONJUNCTIONS (Units 4, 8, 9)

He's very tall **and** handsome. There are four buses **but** one train.
I am tired, **so** Jack is helping me.

NOUNS

NOUN PLURALS (Units 5, 8)

Regular:	bank	orange	bus	countr**y**	church
	bank**s**	orange**s**	bus**es**	countr**ies**	church**es**
Irregular:	child	man	woman	foot	tooth
	child**ren**	m**e**n	wom**e**n	f**ee**t	t**ee**th

COUNT NOUNS/MASS NOUNS (Unit 5)

He's eating **a pear/pears**. He's eating **an apple/apples**.

He's eating **fish**. He's drinking **tea**.

POSSESSIVE OF NOUNS (Units 7, 9)

Whose shirt is this? It's **the boys'/the Browns'**. / **Jack's/Bess's**.

DEFINITE ARTICLE **the**, INDEFINITE ARTICLES **a** and **an**, NO ARTICLE (Units 3, 5)

The tie is on **the** table.
He's eating **a** pear.
He's eating **an** apple.

He's drinking tea.
He's eating pears.
He's eating apples.

CONTRACTIONS (Units 1, 2, 3, 7, 11)

I am—**I'm** he/she is—**he's/she's** we are—**we're**
you are—**you're** it is—**it's** they are—**they're**
what is—**what's** that is—**that's** where is—**where's**
who is—**who's** is not—**isn't** are not—**aren't** can not—**can't**

VERBS

SIMPLE PRESENT **to be** (Units 1, 2, 6)

I **am** Elena Silva.
You **are** a nurse.
He/She **is** an accountant.
It **is** cold.

We
You **are** happy.
They

to be + PREDICATE ADJECTIVE/NOUN (Units 4, 6)

I **am tall**. He **is Japanese**. His hair **is black**.

She **is a doctor**. They **are teachers**.

PRESENT PROGRESSIVE (Units 5, 7)

I **am going** to the supermarket.
You **are buying** bread.
He **is drinking** coffee.
She **is reading** a book.
It **is raining**.

We **are sitting** in the kitchen.
You **are watching** television.
They **are dancing**.

PRESENT PROGRESSIVE IN FUTURE SENSE (Unit 10)

When **are** you **going**? Tomorrow.

PRESENT PROGRESSIVE CONTRASTED WITH SIMPLE PRESENT (Unit 5)

Dick **is** in his room. He**'s sitting** on the bed.

CAN (ABILITY/PERMISSION) (Unit 11)

I **can** swim.
Can you make coffee? No, I **can't**.
Mom, **can** I go to the movies? Yes, you **can**.

HAVE TO/HAS TO (Unit 11)

I/You/We/They **have to** go. He/She **has to** go.

THERE IS/THERE ARE (Unit 8)

There is one train station. **There are** two bus stations.
Is there one library? **Are there** two banks?

STATEMENTS (Unit 1)

His name is Tom. It's Tom.
Joe is wearing a blue hat.

QUESTIONS

YES-NO QUESTIONS (Units 1, 2)

Is his name Tom?

INFORMATION QUESTIONS-QUESTION WORDS (Units 1, 2, 3, 4, 7, 9)

Where are you going?	Where's the tie?
What is he doing?	What's the weather like?
Who is going with you?	Who's this?
When are they coming?	When's the next bus?
Which room is she in?	
How old is he?	
How many lamps are there?	
Whose cup is this?	

CHOICE QUESTIONS (Unit 2)

Is he wearing a blue hat, **or** a red hat?

SHORT ANSWERS (Unit 7)

Yes, I am. No, I'm not.	Yes, it is. No, it isn't.
Yes, you are. No, you're not.	Yes, we are. No, we aren't.
Yes, s(he) is. No, s(he) isn't.	Yes, they are. No, they aren't.

TIME STRUCTURES

PHRASES (Unit 10)

I'm going	**in the afternoon/morning/evening**.	
	at midnight/noon/night.	It's **ten-twenty** (10:20).
	this morning/afternoon.	It's **ten-thirty** (10:30).
	today/tonight/tomorrow/now.	

TIME QUESTIONS (Unit 3)

What time is it?
When is the next bus?

WORD LIST

ANSWERS TO *TEST YOURSELF* SECTIONS

Pp. 21-22.

I. 1. (b) 2. (c) 3. (c) 4. (a), (a) 5. (a) 6. (b) 7. (b) 8. (c) 9. (c) **II.** 1. She's wearing (1, 2, 4, 6, 10, 11, 13). 2. He's wearing (3, 5, 7, 8, 9, 12). **III.** 1. Her name is (....) 2. What's his name? 3. Is his name 4. It's 5. it isn't 6. Who's 7. Is she wearing...?

Pp. 38-39.

I. 1. in 2. in 3. on (under) 4. on (under) 5. on 6. (b) 7. (a) 8. (c) 9. (c) 10. (c) **II.** 1. It's Bill. 2. He's twenty. 3. It's blond. 4. He's thin. 5. They're black. 6. Who's this? 7. What's her last name? 8. How old is she? 9. What color are her eyes? 10. What color is her hair? 11. Is she tall or short? **III.** 1. behind 2. in front of 3. in front of 4. behind

Pp. 61-62

I. 1. (a) 2. (b) 3. (b) 4. (b) 5. (b) 6. (a) 7. (b) **II.** (a, f, k, l, n, o) **III.** 3. a 4. an 5. an 6. a **IV.** 1. Carmen 2. Mexican 3. doctor 4. his nationality 5. How old is he 6. (n) accountant 7. pilot 8. What's John's nationality

Pp. 87-89

I. 1. are 2. am 3. are 4. are 5. (a) 6. (c) **II.** 1. (a) 2. (b) 3. (b) 4. (a) 5. (a) **III.** 1. There is one child. 2. There are three men. 3. There is one woman. 4. There are three feet. 5. There are two babies. 6. There is one church. 7. There are two children. 8. There are four teeth. **IV.** 1. (b) 2. (c) 3. (c) 4. (c) **V.** 1. are they doing 2. are you going 3. many are 4. two men, men here 5. women there 6. libraries 7. we are both tall 8. so am, you are both handsome. **VI.** 1. It's going to the bus station. 2. He's going to the hotel. 3. She's going to the supermarket. 4. He's going to the library. **VII.** 1. you're not (you aren't) 2. I'm not 3. she's not (she isn't) 4. they're not (they aren't)

Pp. 107-108

I. 1. (b) 2. (a) 3. (b) 4. (a) 5. (a) **II.** 1. those 2. that 3. those 4. those 5. This 6. Those 7. these 8. These, those **III.** 1. Whose 2. Whose, They're 3. them to him. 4. it to me 5. Where are you going 6. When are you going 7. Are you 8. Who's going with you 9. two-fifteen 10. eight twenty-five 11. one-thirty (half past one) 12. ten to three

INDEX